THE REIMAGINED CHURCH

HOW TO RETROFIT YOUR CHURCH
TO THRIVE IN THE TWENTY-FIRST
CENTURY AND ENJOY THE JOURNEY.

—Steve Pike with the Next Wave Community

FOREWORD BY DANIEL YANG

THE REIMAGINED CHURCH

BECOMING A CHURCH
THAT WALKS IN THE
WAY OF JESUS

STEVE PIKE

AND THE NEXT WAVE COMMUNITY

EQUIP PRESS

Colorado Springs

THE REIMAGINED CHURCH

Published by Equip Press, Colorado Springs, CO

Cover Design: ArtSpeak Creative

ATTENTION CORPORATIONS, UNIVERSITIES, COLLEGES AND PROFESSIONAL ORGANIZATIONS: Quantity discounts are available on bulk purchases of this book for educational, gift purposes, or as premiums for increasing magazine subscriptions or renewals. Special books or book excerpts can also be created to fit specific needs. For information, please contact Jason Bowman of ArtSpeak Creative at jason@artspeakcreative.com

First Edition: 2024
The Reimagined Church / Steve Pike
Paperback ISBN: 978-1-958585-78-8
eBook ISBN: 978-1-958585-90-0

EQUIP PRESS
Colorado Springs

AUTHOR ACKNOWLEDGEMENTS

Even before the COVID-19 pandemic, it was clear that God had planted seeds for *The Reimagined Church* in the hearts of many church leaders I know and trust. Now that the post-COVID dust is beginning to settle, I hope this book finds the many other church leaders I don't know and gives them a "yes and amen" to their wild, risky, out-of-the-box dreams of building and leading a new kind of church for a new kind of culture.

A very special thanks to all who prayed for, contributed to, and helped shape the direction of this book, specifically our Next Wave Community members Amber and Andrew Gutierrez, Andrew Arrol, Bryce Baldwin, Carl Johnson, Chad Smith, Dr. Charlie Self, Chris May, Danette Ray, Daniel Serdahl, Darius Walden, Donald and Wendy Lott, Dutch VanderVlucht, Eric Hoke, Jarrad Gibler, Jasmine Whiting, Jason Bowman, Jeff Cathey, Jeff Duncan, Jim Moore, Joe Bridger, Johnny Taylor, Joshua Jamison, Kylie Roberts, Larry Grawey, LaWayne Swartzel, Mark Johnson, Mark Taylor, Matthew Collver, Max Souza, Michael James Mella, Morris Pike, Paul Durbin, Sergio Acedo, Taylor Carmicle, Tobey Montgomery, and Uriah Fracassi.

This work is *truly* a group effort. My prayer is for the future of the twenty-first-century Church to be undergirded with the same camaraderie and shared wisdom found between the pages of this book.

CONTENTS

FOREWORD

IN 2017, I MOVED TO Chicagoland to start and lead what is now the Church Multiplication Institute at the Wheaton College Billy Graham Center. Until that point, most of the ministry books I read focused on helping pastors navigate local church ministry or think better about culture and society. Although I was immersed in the world of church planting, I wasn't yet fully exposed to the world of church network leadership and organizational consulting—a ministry space that advocated the Biblical reasons for church planting but also seemed stuck in an industrial model of church planting. I realized in the first few months of leading the institute that while, at this level of leadership, there was an evangelistic motivation for starting new churches, what impacted most the kinds of churches being planted were the processes, systems, and structures of church planting. As the church in America was entering the second decade of the twenty-first century, I started to sense that we weren't seeing innovative and evangelistically effective churches started because our church planting structure was set and built around the best practices of forty years ago, which was also predicated on the golden age of the church in America coming out of World War II.

About six months into leading the institute, I stumbled upon *Leading Church Multiplication*, written by Tom Nebel and Steve Pike. It was the first book I ever read focused on those who lead church planters and church planting organizations. It provided me with the concepts and language I needed in order to connect with and better serve network leaders through the work of the institute. I distinctly remember two things as I finished the book: 1) I realized that I had a steep learning curve when it came to serving network leaders because I had only led in a local church context, and 2) if we're going to see a new generation of leaders emerge on mission, then we must change the narratives and structures—the imagination—around church and church planting in North America.

Shortly after this realization, Steve and I connected over email. I was doing a research project on church planting systems, and Ed Stetzer told me I needed to talk to Steve. Steve started the Church Multiplication Network of the Assemblies of God, which became one of the largest church planting networks in America. After about a decade of leading the network, Steve transitioned it to a younger leader so he could start something new and different called Urban Islands Project. In the world of church planting, Steve is a pioneer, practitioner, and patriarch! In the world of missional leadership in denominational life, Steve was at the top. But he had stepped away from those roles to imagine something different and more creative than the industrial model.

I think Steve would be the first to tell you that God is doing amazing things through Urban Islands, but it isn't the silver bullet or the only way to think about the future of mission and church planting in America. But he is doing something that I see only a handful of others doing—as a proven leader in the prevailing model of church planting, he is courageously helping both traditional church leaders and never-seen-before church leaders hope and dream for a next wave of missional leaders. Not only is Steve casting a vision for the future of the church through his books and training, but he's stepped out once again as a practitioner and pioneer to provide a model—a new imagination—for others to build.

The future of the church in America does not depend on a model or a process or system. The future of the church in America will be created by those who wholly trust in God and are hearing and obeying the voice of Jesus. This posture necessitates that we honor and respect how God has moved in the past through what we now consider to be traditional or prevailing models. The church on mission always has continuity with the church in history. However, trusting God and obeying Jesus' voice in the twenty-first century will not look like what happened during the 1950s during the golden age of Christian denominationalism or the 1990s during the height of the Church Growth Movement or the early 2000s when missional church took off in America. It will have some continuity, but it will look and feel different.

Steve and other leaders like him are challenging, and maybe even double-dog daring, today's missional and network leaders to dream and do something different than what the leaders before already did so well. He's asking many of us to stand on their shoulders so that the Kingdom of God can go further. And I haven't asked him this, but I suspect that if all who worked with him were just trying to plant the same kinds of churches we've been planting for the last forty years, reaching only the same kinds of people we've been reaching, he might feel a little discouraged. But I think what he's doing with Urban Islands Project, *The Next Wave*, and *The Reimagined Church* is to prophetically say, "You can do it, and you must do it!"

For the sake of Jesus' name, and the sake of those who don't yet know Him, my prayer is that we do it because we must do it.

— *Daniel Yang*
Former Director of the Church Multiplication Institute
at Wheaton College Billy Graham Center

When you experience the joy of leading a church through a successful process of reimagination, it will be worth every challenge you've had to overcome because the outcome of a reimagined church is a community of disciples vigorously walking with Jesus on His Mission. It's setting in motion a movement of transformation that is as irresistible and unstoppable as the Mission of Jesus Himself. Are you ready to be part of a miracle? Let's go!

—Steve Pike

NOW WHAT?

How does the Church thrive in this post-COVID-19 world?

The Parable of Pastor Pat

Let me introduce you to Pastor Pat. Pat is a ministry everyman. He's a middle-aged, veteran church leader doing the best he can to surf the crashing waves of the rapidly evolving twenty-first-century cultural context. Pat is married with a couple of kids. He does his best to be a good father and husband. He's a team player, is loyal to his denomination, and yet reserves the right to think for himself. His favorite ways to learn are books and podcasts. Pat now finds himself leading a struggling church whose demise seems to be painfully inevitable.

Pat is not at all happy. His denominational leaders had decided to place him in a fifty-year-old church made up of a group of generally disgruntled parishioners whose average age was seventy+. The only thing they had going for them was a decent building in an acceptable location. Otherwise, the church seemed destined to be closed within a decade. The thought of passively presiding over the slow, painful demise of a formerly great church made Pat feel sick to his stomach.

Surely this wasn't the way God intended for him to live out his prime ministry years.

Even in the best of times, leading this particular church through change would be a challenge. Now, facing the twin giants of a rapidly evolving culture and the seemingly endless ongoing impacts of the COVID-19 epidemic, helping this church discover a viable future felt like an impossible dream. So much of what he had been taught in seminary seemingly no longer applied. Most of the existing parishioners just wanted their church to stay the same. They had no interest in making any significant changes to restore the church to missional vitality.

But Pat was not content to preside over a slowly sinking ship. He longed to see a thriving church that effectively made the power and presence of Jesus known in every nook and cranny of culture and society. "Yeah, but how?" he wondered.

The Story of Bethel Temple

As we momentarily leave Pastor Pat to process his next steps, let's take a quick excursion back to 1969 in Canton, Ohio. Bethel Temple Church. Song Leader Tommy Ferguson enthusiastically invites the gathered congregation to sing exuberant songs of worship to the Lord. "Turn with me to page 216, and let's sing together verses one, two, and four." (For some reason, we often skipped verse three of most songs). The pianist and the organist blended their harmonious chords together, providing a dramatic instrumental introduction building to the point where the congregational voices would join in. Tommy is behind a massive light oak pulpit, and behind him is a robed choir following his every cue. Between Tommy and the choir, the pastoral team is seated wearing suits, ties, and contagious smiles. The sanctuary is brightly lit by overhead lighting and massive opaque windows designed to let the sunshine in. The congregants are dressed in their Sunday best, from the youngest to the oldest. Everyone is holding a hard-bound hymnal stamped with the title "Hymns of Glorious Praise." Bethel Temple in September 1969 was the embodiment of what everyone knew a great church should be. Little did we know, this culturally appropriate scene was about to be swept away by a fresh wave of the Spirit known as the Jesus Movement.

Fast forward to Bethel Temple 1976. Tommy Ferguson has been replaced by a "worship team" of guitar-strumming minstrels wearing jeans. The congregation is a complex mix of folks dressed up in their Sunday "go-to-meeting" clothes and a diverse assortment of younger people not wearing suits, ties, and dresses. Some of the older members are unhappy with how "their church" has been hijacked by the newcomers. But, for the most part, the church has successfully caught the wave of the Jesus Movement and is thriving in a brave new world.

I know this story because Bethel Temple was my church—the church my family and I attended while I was in high school. I lived through this transition and experienced the joys and the tensions directly. I saw first-hand the disturbed looks on the faces of some of my elders when I showed up to church wearing jeans. I felt the exhilaration of worshipping with new songs birthed out of the radical transformation of young seekers. Watching the church I grew up in navigate her way through a cultural upheaval gives me hope that any church can successfully ride the towering cultural wave that is now crashing around us.

Indeed, the church we all knew in 2019 is being battered by the unanticipated and ongoing disruption of COVID-19. The next church is beginning to emerge as an increasingly fragmented version of its former somewhat homogeneous self.

That pre-COVID-19 version of the church looked something like this:

> The friendly greeters welcome the regulars and their guests as they make their way into the carefully curated worship space. The lack of windows prevents any natural light from spoiling the visual experience carefully controlled from the massive production booth at the rear of the room. The preservice playlist is cranking, and the perfectly formatted slides inform the incoming participants of the upcoming opportunities for connection, worship, training, and service. At precisely the appointed moment, the fog begins to flow, and the music swells as the live worship band rallies the troops for praise. The synchronized lighting pulses to the beat of the music with a level of quality that rivals world-class music acts. As the worship set draws to a close, the announcement video seamlessly keeps the program moving forward, setting up the moment when the pastor steps to the stage and holds the audience spellbound for the next twenty-five minutes using a combination of artistic graphics and carefully chosen words. The worship band helps wrap up the experience with an anthem for the ages. The congregation departs with optimism, hope, and joy, ready to face another week in the real world.

Like her 1969 counterpart, this common pre-COVID-19 version of the church represented what everyone knew a great church should be. And like her 1969 counterpart, the pre-COVID-19 version of the church in her attempt to embrace the "old normal," is in danger of being swept away. The question on the minds of every church leader who cares about faithfully following Jesus on His mission in this new reality is "Now what?"

"Now what?" is the question that this book attempts to answer. The members of the Next Wave Community and I are suggesting that the optimum way forward is to "reimagine" the church. But before we think about what reimagining looks like, let's explore the other popular options for responding to the disruption. By the way, COVID-19 only accelerated a huge wave that was already bearing down on the North American church. The disruption is not just about COVID-19 but about a whole new worldview that has changed the church's playing field. Every church has responded to this emerging new reality in some way. We're suggesting that the observed responses fall into three general categories. Reopen. Relaunch. Reimagine.

The Reopen Option

Leaders and churches who have chosen to "reopen" have decided the best way forward is to return as soon as possible to doing exactly what they were doing pre-COVID-19. This option has a lot of support from the most faithful and most financially consistent churchgoers. Honestly, it's the easiest and perhaps even the most logical option. Nothing new to learn. Those who come back are pleased to find everything just as they left it. It feels like most church attendees will choose this option over any of the alternatives.

The challenge with the reopen approach is that early trends indicate not everyone is coming back. Researchers, like our friends at the Church Multiplication Institute[1], report that, on average, about 1/3 of the previous active, engaged attendees are coming back as active, engaged attendees. Another 1/3 are coming back but are only occasional attendees

---

1   Daniel Yang, Executive Director of the Church Multiplication Institute, In person presentation the Church Planting Leadership Fellowship meeting in Brentwood, TN on Wednesday, November 15, 2023.

and tend to be much less engaged than they were in the pre-COVID-19 version of the church. Another 1/3 are most likely not coming back if "coming back" means attending face-to-face gatherings.

The other challenge with exercising the "reopen" option is the reality of the average life expectancy of a church. According to research by David Olson and The American Church Research Project, a study of 90,000 churches from 2007–2008 revealed that "established churches that were over forty years old, on average, declined in attendance."[2] Obviously, there will be exceptions, but the big data points to the reality that older churches tend to lose their missional momentum. The implication is that, without intervention, the church you lead will begin to face serious missional headwinds as it enters its fourth decade. Reopening will not reset the trend toward missional impotency. It will take you one step closer to the inevitable.

The Relaunch Option

Leaders and churches that choose to "relaunch" recognize the once-in-a-lifetime opportunity that COVID-19 has provided for the church. They see the disruption as an opportunity to look at everything they were doing before COVID-19 and ask some powerful questions like—What were we doing before COVID-19 that we should not start up again? What did we start during COVID-19 that we should continue to do?

The result is similar to what happens when someone chooses to remodel a house. The basic infrastructure is left in place, but new fixtures and design features that make the house more livable are installed. Old and outdated wallpaper is replaced with trendy color schemes. Bathrooms

---

2   David T. Olson, *The American Church in Crisis* (Grand Rapids, Michigan: Zondervan, 2008), page 83.

and kitchens are given a makeover. Perhaps a completely new room is added to accommodate newer technologies.

Relaunching is a great option for many existing churches. The disruption of COVID-19 has provided a unique opportunity to set in motion a relaunching process. It allows a church to shed traditions and habits that were no longer helping them be with Jesus on His Mission. Money that had been tied up in missionally fruitless efforts can be redirected toward strategically targeted missional endeavors.

The challenge with the relaunch option is that when all of the dust settles, a relaunched church may be just more of the same, dressed up in different attire. They may be a better version of themselves, but are they the expression of the Church needed in the challenging new cultural context in which we find ourselves? Are they still measuring missional momentum with unhelpful metrics? Are they doomed to slowly drift toward missional irrelevance because they are answering questions no one is asking?

All things considered, depending on the circumstances, reopening and relaunching may be acceptable short-term responses to the COVID-19 disruption. However, this book is about the "reimagined" church. Reimagining is very different from reopening or relaunching. Churches that choose to pursue a strategy of reimagining recognize that the forms of the twentieth-century church are woefully inadequate for the robust challenges of the twenty-first-century context. They recognize that twentieth-century church forms have a relatively short shelf life—perhaps twenty years at the most. The twenty-first-century cultural context is obliterating twentieth-century forms of the church in front of our eyes. Reopening or relaunching will only delay the onset of the inevitable.

Reopening and relaunching strategies mirror the way many coastal communities are currently responding to rising sea levels. In a *New*

York Times article entitled "Miami Says It Can Adapt to Rising Seas. Not Everyone Is Convinced," authors Christopher Flavelle and Patricia Mazzei describe the civic efforts in Miami to deal with the rising sea levels that have become all too real.

> Officials in Miami-Dade County, where climate models predict two feet or more of sea-level rise by 2060, have released an upbeat strategy for living with more water, one that focused on elevating homes and roads, more dense construction farther inland, and creating more open space for flooding in low-lying areas.
>
> That blueprint, made public on Friday, portrayed rising seas as mostly manageable, especially for a low-lying area with a century of experience managing water.
>
> Climate experts, though, warned that the county's plan downplayed the magnitude of the threat, saying it failed to warn residents and developers about the risk of continuing to build near the coast in a county whose economy depends heavily on waterfront real estate."[3]

What's happening in Miami-Dade County—the denial, the overconfidence, the self-deception, and more—has a perfect parallel in the American church right now. The sea level of twenty-first-century culture is rising beyond anything previously experienced. Twentieth-century church culture portrays the challenge as "mostly manageable,"

3   Christopher Flavelle and Patricia Mazzei, "Miami Says It Can Adapt to Rising Seas. Not Everyone Is Convinced," New York Times, March 2, 2021, https://www.nytimes.com/2021/03/02/climate/miami-sea-level-rise.html

while the prophets and apostles of the Church are warning of the impending doom. We seem to be content to tweak what we've been doing.

Hippocrates may have coined the phrase "desperate times call for desperate measures." It's the appropriate phrase for the rising tide of twenty-first-century culture. Tweaking what we've been doing will only lead to a relentless cycle of tweaking that, in the end, may be washed away by the irresistible inundation of culture coming our way. The only way forward is complete reimagination. For the residents of Miami-Dade County, that may mean replacing their streets with waterways and their foundations with floating platforms. For leaders of the Church, it will mean replacing cherished practices that have become detached from the virulent mission of Jesus with newly discovered ways of joining Jesus to seek and save the lost.

A Third Way—the Reimagine Option

The purpose of this book is to provide a framework for "reimagining" the church. Fair warning—reimagining is not the path of least resistance. In fact, reimagining is much more difficult than starting a church from scratch. Leading a congregation through a complete reimagination of itself will take more than a sermon series, campaign, or rebranding process. Existing churches often have layers of resistance to change that have built up over the years. Processing through the resistance to change takes time, patience, wisdom, tenacity, and a crystal-clear vision of the destination that the leader has never seen before. The pathway to reimagination is fraught with distractions, holy cows, and scary moments. The flurry of church activities or the physicality of church buildings creates a mirage of tangibility that makes existing churches feel solid. People like what they know and tenaciously resist change. Indeed, in a Fast Company article entitled "Change or Die," author Alan Deutschman shares the truth about how the majority of humans respond to a challenge to change their ways—nine out of ten times, they say, "Thanks, but no thanks."[4]

Let the reader proceed with no illusions then—guiding a church through the process of reimagination will challenge every fiber of the leadership bones in your body. You'll be tried, tested, questioned, criticized, and even vilified—all by people you thought were your friends. You'll wonder why you ever messed with the way things were. You'll think perhaps the church you left behind wasn't that bad after all. My point is this—do not embark on this journey without carefully and comprehensively counting the cost.

Know that even when you've counted the cost, there is no guarantee you will be successful. However, if you experience the joy of leading a church through a successful process of reimagination, it will be worth every challenge you've had to overcome because the outcome of a reimagined church is a community of disciples vigorously walking with Jesus on His Mission. It's setting in motion a movement of transformation as irresistible and unstoppable as the Mission of Jesus Himself. Are you ready to be part of a miracle? Let's go!

How to Reimagine Your Church

Ready for a quick flyover of the reimagine process?

1. Be the Change. It starts with you. You'll need to be the change before anyone else will be changed.

2. Destination. Begin with the end in mind.

---

4   Alan Dueschman, Fast Company Website, "Change or Die," May 1, 2005. https://www.fastcompany.com/52717/change-or-die

3. Lifecycle. Know your personal and organizational lifecycle.

4. Expect. Not everyone will make the switch.

5. Focus. Go with the Goers.

6. Stabilize. The power of both/and.

7. Experiment. Try stuff. Joyfully failing forward.

8. Empower. Leverage the power of distributed leadership

9. Visionize. Envision the future with the Goers.

10. Patience. Give the process time to work.

11. Steady. Don't waver. Long obedience in the same direction

12. Celebrate. Measure what matters and party a lot.

The church you lead does not inevitably need to wander down the path of painful, slow decline. But it will not find its way forward with Jesus without intentional intervention. That's what this book is about—intentional intervention that breaks the cycle of content and joyously joins Jesus wherever he may lead.

Change CAN happen!

Don't Reimagine Alone. Do It with a Community.

The reimagine process isn't one man's work or ideas. It's the result of a collective effort from dozens of global church leaders, their experiences with COVID-19 ministry, and how they overcame old-model challenges to continue reaching people with the good news of Jesus.

And they didn't need to live in the same city or walk the same streets to collaborate on a new paradigm for ministry. They built the reimagine process together—entirely online—in the Next Wave Community.

The Next Wave Community is an online community where church leaders from around the world gather for daily discussion, prayer, and support. Each week, the community meets on Zoom to participate in a lively conversation with leaders like Mark Batterson, Alan Hirsch, Ralph Moore, and other effective innovators you've probably never heard of.

The Next Wave Community is real-time learning, innovation, and community, no matter where you are. Don't reimagine alone. Join the Next Wave Community today using the QR code below.

PART ONE

GET READY

CHAPTER ONE

BE THE CHANGE
You've Got to Be It to Lead It

"Setting an example is not the main means of influencing others; it is the only means."

–ALBERT EINSTEIN

The Parable of Pastor Pat

"Transitions in ministry duties are a great time for ministry leaders to pause and reflect on what they've learned so far." Pastor Pat read that quote in an article published in a ministry journal. It bugged him. He had never enjoyed pausing to authentically reflect. Reflection always made him aware of his shortcomings and failures. He didn't like climbing down the rabbit hole of any sort of introspection. His instinct was to bulldoze ahead and run full speed into his next ministry assignment, confident that the lessons he'd learned along the way so far would bring him success in his new position of responsibility.

But this time felt different. His familiar, confident outlook on life was being challenged in ways he'd never experienced before. Even if the church was a thriving ministry juggernaut with maximum positive momentum, it seemed to Pat that the buffeting headwinds of culture would make the next season of ministry unusually challenging. But the church was anything but a "ministry juggernaut." Leading this particular church into the unknown of the future felt like a giant Pat had never faced thus far in his ministry journey. He pondered, "Am I the right person to lead this church right now? Am I the right person to lead ANY church right now?"

WE'RE STARTING HERE BECAUSE IF you don't get this right, leading your organization through change is impossible. Reimagining the church starts with you—the leader. Leading a church through the complex process of catching the wave of twenty-first-century culture means the habits and behaviors of the church will have to change. In most cases, this means that YOU will have to change. Personal change cannot be delegated to another staff member, team, or committee. If the church you lead is going to successfully catch this next wave, you must lead by example first. If you don't, then you are not the leader!

Seriously—we've all seen the fallout of leaders whose motto appears to be "Do as I say, not as I do." Faithful followers assume that the daily actions of their leader are in complete congruence with the daily words of their leaders. In the worst cases, those close to the leaders see the disparity between words and deeds but overlook it because they reason that the positive good accomplished by the leader through their inspiring words is more important than personal integrity. And so followers are inspired and honor the great leader until one day, the curtain is pulled back, the discrepancies between the words and deeds are exposed, and it is one hot mess. You know the names. You fill in the blanks. We don't want this to happen to you.

The antidote to this is living life as an open book in clear view of all. Jesus is exhibit A. You need look no further than God in the Flesh for what this looks like in real life. If anyone ever had the right to live above and beyond His followers, it was Jesus. He was literally from "above and beyond." But as we know, he emptied himself and showed us how to lead by being a servant. The Kingdom he revealed is completely backward from what we expect. The creator of the universe is born in a stable, not a palace. The Lord of All Creation demonstrates his lordship by washing the feet of his followers—a role reserved for servants. Do you see a leadership theme emerging here?

Following Jesus faithfully leaves no room for pompous posers masquerading as Kingdom leaders. Kingdom leaders live real life in proximity to those they lead. Here's the point. To help the church you lead work its way through a process of reimagination, you must be willing to lead like Jesus. Up close and personal.

The Leadership Style of Jesus

In his excellent book *The Servant*, author James Hunter unpacks the leadership style of Jesus by suggesting an exercise that exposes the core of how Jesus led. Participants are asked to think about the leaders they've followed who have led well. They are then invited to reflect on the characteristics of those leaders.

We invite the reader to take a moment to ponder the same question. What were the characteristics of the leaders who have led you well? Think back on your actual experiences and make a list of the characteristics that come to mind.

We will come back to your list in a bit, but first, let's think together about the core personal characteristics of Jesus that we are called to imitate. Before we are leaders, we are people. Luke tells us that, as a person, Jesus grew in wisdom, stature, favor with God, and favor within his culture.[1] Here, we are presented with four spaces of life that Jesus was intentional about growing in and the Gospel writer was intentional in telling us about. Before we worry about how our leadership style aligns with the leadership style of Jesus, let's dive into the formation of Jesus.

Four Ways That Jesus Thrived:

Wisdom: Intellectual Well-Being

The Merriam-Webster Dictionary says that wisdom is "knowledge that is gained by having many experiences in life." Wisdom goes deeper than just having philosophical ideas or knowing data-based facts. Wisdom is understanding how philosophical concepts and empirical facts are best applied in real-life situations. The scriptures are mostly silent regarding what Jesus was doing in the first thirty years of his life, but Luke lets us know that he was growing in wisdom. Wisdom grows when we pay attention to the experiences of life and learn from them.

Having a high wisdom quotient is a crucial characteristic of the leader who will guide the reimagining process well because the reimagining process will be fraught with unexpected twists and turns coming from every imaginable direction:

1. People who say they want to change but really don't mean it

2. Experiments that don't go well and fuel the fire of the naysayers

3. Zealous change agents who scare people

4. Scared obstructionists who want to recapture the good old days

---

1   Luke 2:52 (NIV)

Without a leader acting wisely, every reimagine effort is doomed to fail.

So how do we cultivate wisdom?

1. **Ask.** Yes, Solomon prayed for it. Jesus grew in it. We are explicitly told to ask for it. "If any of you lacks wisdom, you should ask God, who gives generously to all without finding fault, and it will be given to you."[2]

2. **Harvest** wisdom from your own past experiences. Pause to reflect on leadership experiences from your past. What did you get right? What did you get wrong? What could you have done differently? Deliberately learning from your past experiences is how wisdom is built.

3. **Learn** from the experiences of others. Wise leaders learn from the best practices and mistakes of others.

Stature: Physical Well-Being

Jesus was fully God incarnated as a fully human person. He had a real physical body. He deliberately chose to become, as the Joan Osborne song says, "a slob like one of us."[3] His physicality is not incidental. It is intentional.

In the same way, our bodies are not just an incidental add either. The stewardship of our physical bodies is directly connected to our spiritual formation and emotional well-being. We simply don't have the luxury of ignoring the relationship between our body, soul, and spirit. They

2   James 1:15 (NIV)

3   "One Of Us" from the Album *Relish*, written by Eric Bazillion and sung by Joan Osborne, Published by Warner Chappell Music, Inc., 1996.

all impact each other. It's unrealistic to think that what happens to our bodies has no impact on the state of our soul and spirit.

This is why healthy twenty-first-century leaders who initiate the process of church reimagination will be deliberate about stewarding their physical bodies well. We will stop short of prescribing some sort of physical fitness regimen, but here are some very pragmatic steps to take to help your physical body be up to the reimagination task.

1. **Sleep well**. For some bizarre reason, many church leaders take pride in burning the candle at both ends—up super early for prayer, studying late into the night, and busily shepherding the flock nonstop all day long. Prayer and study are important, but good sleep makes the prayer and study go further faster.

2. **Eat well**. A walk through the hallway of any gathering of church leaders may cause one to ask whether gluttony is a desired virtue for Christian leadership. Do some research and be intentional about fueling your body with food that gives energy and promotes health.

3. **Move**! Deliberately incorporate movement into your daily rhythms. It may indeed feel like a challenge when so much of church leadership involves sitting down to counsel, study, meet, travel, and gather. Find ways to stand up and move. (A friend had a treadmill installed in his office so he could walk on the treadmill during phone calls.)

Favor with God: Spiritual Well-Being

Counterintuitively, this is the area in which most spiritual leaders feel the highest degree of confidence, yet, in reality, this may be the weakest link of the four ways Jesus thrived. It's a huge potential blind spot because so much of spiritual leaders' time is spent doing "spiritual" things—praying, reading the Word, studying for sermons, answering spiritual questions, etc. At the end of a long day of ministry, it's easy to take for granted that the spiritual health of the spiritual leader is intact. Until it's not. Then, too often, it's too late.

Gauging your spiritual health quotient. (a non-exhaustive evaluation inventory)

- How are you deliberately listening to and obeying prompts of the Spirit daily?
- How frequently are you carving out time separate from sermon prep where you allow the Word of God to challenge you and choose to act on the challenge?
- How are you habitually carrying on a conversation with God throughout the day?
- How are you soliciting feedback from those who are closest to you? Your spouse, your kids, your friends, your team members, your staff members? What are they seeing that you are not?
- How are you learning from other leaders about the tangible things they do to maintain their own spiritual vitality?

Honestly consider your answers to the questions above and take appropriate actions to keep your spiritual well-being vibrant.

Favor within Your Culture: Emotional and Social Well-Being

In 1995, Daniel Goleman wrote the book *Emotional Intelligence* and catalyzed an entire industry around the notion that part of the makeup of great leaders was cultivating and having high emotional intelligence. "…Goleman defines emotional intelligence as 'the ability to recognize, assess, control, and utilize your own emotions, and those of others.' In his book, he says that this is an underlying factor in being more successful in life."[4]

More recently, Pastor Peter Scazzero has provided an incredibly valuable leadership resource through the release of his book "The Emotionally Healthy Leader." In the book, Peter shares the brutally transparent story of his own journey toward emotional health by taking us on a journey through what he calls four conversions. 1. From Agnosticism to Zealous Christian Leader. 2. From Emotional Blindness to Emotional Health. 3. From Busy Activity to Slowed-Down Spirituality. 4. From Skimming to Integrity in Leadership.

Taking stock of your emotional and social well-being is a non-negotiable step toward determining your readiness to lead a reimagination process because the emotional and social dimensions of your life will be tested like never before. You'll be questioned, challenged, accused, gossiped about, disrespected, ignored, second-guessed, undermined, and rejected. Longtime friends will walk away. The lack of loyalty will catch you off guard. If you start this journey with your emotional tank near empty, you will quickly find yourself stranded and alone.

Do yourself a favor. Find a consultant qualified to take you through an Emotional Intelligence Assessment. Learn from the results and take the time to develop any necessary new habits. Read, process, and take action on Pete Scazzero's book to raise your awareness of the status of your personal emotional health.

---

4   Success Quarterly Website, "How Daniel Goleman Define Emotional
     Intelligence," 2024, accessed March 1, 2024. https://successquarterly.com/how-
     daniel-goleman-define-emotional-intelligence/

The Motive That Makes It All Work

Ok, remember the list we started? It's time to come back to that. The question was, "What are the characteristics of leaders who have led you well?" Here are some of the answers other people have shared. "They cared about me as a person." "They intentionally provided opportunities for me to grow." "They were patient with my mistakes." "They tangibly demonstrated interest in my family." "They acted with integrity." "They sacrificed for the good of their employees." "They listened to my ideas." "They celebrated my success." "They enjoyed the journey." "They didn't give up on me."

Notice what is not on your list or the sample list above. "They made me feel small." "Everything was always all about them." "They always had to have the last word on everything." "They were insecure." "They were jealous." "They made me feel unsafe." "I was afraid of them." "They acted like I didn't matter or even exist."

Now go back to your list and the sample list from others. Does it sound familiar? Do you get the sense that you've seen this list someplace before?

How about this list of characteristics of good leaders? Good leaders are patient, kind, not jealous, not boastful, not proud, not dishonoring of others, not self-seeking, not easily angered, not scorekeepers, unhappy with injustice, encouraged by justice, protective, trusting, hopeful, tenacious, and never quit.

You're right. You know where that list comes from. 1 Corinthians 13. The so-called "Love" chapter.

"Love is patient, love is kind. It does not envy, it does not boast, it is not proud. It does not dishonor others, it is not self-seeking, it is not easily angered, it keeps no record of wrongs. Love does not delight in evil but rejoices with the truth. It always protects, always trusts, always hopes, always perseveres. Love never fails" (1 Corinthians 13:4-8).

Isn't that interesting? Turns out that love is the core motive of the leaders we've been led well by. The underlying motive of a leader is more important than the "style" of the leader. The underlying motive is what makes the style work or not. It's a popular notion that the "best" leadership style is "collaborative." While that is often true, some situations demand other leadership styles. For example, in an emergency situation, the most loving leadership style is not collaborative! Fire in the building likely requires a commanding leadership approach.

Norwich University suggests that there are ten leadership styles.[5] Visionary, Coaching, Affiliative, Democratic, Pacesetting, Autocratic, Commanding, Laissez-faire, Bureaucratic, and Servant. A quick flyover of the Gospels allows us to see Jesus using all these styles.

Visionary – I will build my Church.

Coaching – What did you learn as you went?

Affiliative – You are my disciples.

Democratic – You feed them.

Pacesetting – This is how everyone will know you are my disciples.

Autocratic – If you love me, do what I say.

Commanding – Go and make disciples.

Laissez-faire – Jesus slept while the storm raged.

Bureaucratic – Who do you say that I am?

Servant – He washed their feet.

---

5   Norwich University, "10 Different Types of Leadership Styles," accessed March 1, 2024. https://online.norwich.edu/academic-programs/resources/10-different-types-leadership-styles

The styles change, but the core motive doesn't. That's what makes all the leadership styles effective. Healthy leaders will tend to shift from style to style depending on the situation. But what will make them all effective is the core motive of love.

Energy and Motivation

One more thing to think about. In the third chapter of this book, we will consider the impact of the lifecycle of a church on the blueprint of your reimagination strategy. But this chapter is about you, and you have a lifecycle too. For purposes of this discussion, let's define lifecycle as the energy and motivation you have at any given time. Leading a church through a process of reimagining is extremely difficult. The leader needs high levels of both energy and motivation to successfully lead a church on the reimagination journey. This crucial consideration deserves a serious assessment of your readiness to lead.

If you are at a place in your life where you are experiencing low energy (perhaps due to illness or fatigue) and low motivation (perhaps you are unclear as to why the church needs to be reimagined), now is NOT the time to take on a reimagination project. Definite red light.

This pause to reflect on your personal readiness may even result in the realization that it might be time to step aside and allow another leader to guide the church through the reimagination process. Please don't be THAT leader who stays too long for whatever reason!

A caution light might be appropriate if you have either low energy/ high motivation or high energy/low motivation. Proceed with great caution, and don't commit until your energy and motivation levels are high.

Even if your energy is off the charts and your motivation is strong, be sure you take the time to assess how aligned you are with the leadership model of Jesus.

Here's why all this matters. If you want to successfully lead a church through a process of reimagining herself, you've got to start with yourself. Glaring character flaws and persistent insecurities will ultimately sabotage your reimagination efforts. Now, before you take any more tangible steps down the path of reimagination, is the time to assess your leadership health and take the necessary actions to deal with significant issues in your leadership wheelhouse. Prepare yourself so you are ready to lead others well.

Once you've reached a point of confidence that you are the right leader to oversee the reimagination process, it's time to get started! But where to begin? We recommend you begin at the end!

Beginning at the end will be the subject of our next chapter.

> *Jump into the Next Wave Community to meet other leaders who can help you assess your leadership health. Join the Next Wave Community today using the QR code below.*

CHAPTER TWO

DESTINATION
Beginning with the End in Mind

The Parable of Pastor Pat

After spending some time in deep reflection regarding his personal readiness for leading a church through a reimagination process, Pastor Pat felt that he was called by God and might be up to the task. But what exactly was the task? The existing members of the church claimed they wanted revival. Pat wasn't sure what that meant to them. His denominational leaders wanted him to revitalize the church. When he asked them what they meant by that, their answer was ambiguous and cryptic—"We want to see the church growing and thriving." "Ok…" Pat thought, "What in the world does that mean?"

He himself wanted to do more than just maintain the status quo. He sensed a personal yearning to nurture a church culture that was deeper and richer than any church he'd previously led or been a part of. "What is God guiding me to do? Where is God wanting this church to go?" "How can I know?"

You've undoubtedly heard the message loud and clear that this process of reimagining the church will not be the path of least resistance. This journey isn't a quick fix for the things that bug you about your church! It will likely be a meandering journey—with setbacks and surprises, moments of joy interspersed with seasons of discouragement and second-guessing. It's actually a lot like climbing a mountain.

Having lived near mountains for nearly half my life, I've climbed a few and learned along the way that every mountain climb is a metaphor for accomplishing anything hard in life. The first few steps of any climb are invigorating. The trail is clearly marked, the air is fresh, the legs are willing, and the shade of the trees is cool and energizing.

As you ascend, the trail becomes less clear, the air becomes thinner, the legs begin talking back to you, and the trees begin to disappear. Further on, near the summit, there is no trail, the lungs scream for air, the legs weigh one thousand pounds each, and there are no trees—only craggy, relentless rocks between you and the goal. You press on, one lead-filled foot in front of the other, tenaciously moving toward the reason you are enduring all this pain. Ironically, for most of the journey, you can't even see the top of the mountain. What keeps you going? The picture seared in your brain of the magnificent summit. You know that if you turn back, you won't experience the joy of standing triumphantly on the pinnacle of the peak, surrounded by a vast, unobstructed vista. In mountain climbing, it's the end that keeps us going.

But which peak are we climbing? This requires the climbing party to agree on the peak that will be their destination. This common destination keeps the climbers together and helps them avoid the perils of climbing the mountain alone.

When climbing a mountain, ambiguity about the destination can be deadly. Lack of a clear destination for a reimagine process can be just as dangerous. Yet it happens all the time. A leader confidently stands before his assembled team and makes a generic declaration about the destination. Everyone nods their head in agreement and affirms with sincere-sounding "Amens." Months later, the team has exploded into divided factions going in different directions. The most common cause of disunity is a lack of agreement regarding where the group is going— what peak are we actually climbing?

Starting with an agreed-upon destination reduces the risks on the mountain of reimagination. Having the picture of the preferred future seared in your brain and tattooed on your heart will keep you headed in the right direction as you put one foot in front of the other. Without a clear picture of where God is taking you, you will drift off the path and end up in a valley you might not want to be in. So it is essential, as Stephen Covey would say, to "start with the end in mind." [6]

How to Start with the End in Mind

In this chapter, we will explore the five steps to determining your destination. Let's think of this as the trail map to the top of the mountain.

1. Listening prayer

2. Scripture-centered motivation

3. A guiding framework

4. A commitment to see the process through

5. A clear and compelling picture of your destination

---

6 Stephen Covey, *The 7 Habits of Highly Effective People* (New York, NY: Simon & Schuster, 1984, 2004).

The Five Steps to the End

Step One – Listening Prayer

Since the picture of the destination must come from the heart of God, the starting place for seeking that picture is through listening to what the Spirit is saying. The reimagined church process does not begin with a discussion among church leaders, reading the same book together, or a confident declaration from the visionary leader (although the process often includes all of these actions).

The reimagined church process starts with a season of listening carefully to the One who is building His Church. We humbly come to Jesus with open hands and a surrendered heart willing to lay aside the habits and traditions of "church as it is" and a willingness to take up the challenge of being the "church that will be."

How do we hear His voice as we prayerfully lean into this new season of reimagination? We return to scripture. A provocative definition of a disciple of Jesus is simply a person who recognizes the voice of Jesus—and obeys His voice. Reading the Gospels slowly in community and then together doing what Jesus asks us to do is core to reimagining a Jesus-centered congregation.

Step Two – Scripture-Centered Motivation

A significant guidepost for discerning the destination is giving scripture—and the voice of Jesus in the Gospels—pride of place. This is, after all, the church that Jesus is building. We need to make sure we are joining Him in what He is doing—not just inviting Him to bless all the creative ideas we want to try out. Our motivation for reimagining must be firmly anchored to these Jesus-centric scriptural principles.

Here are some common motives we've observed that are NOT rooted in scripture:

- The desire to "grow" the church for the sake of growth. This can be tricky to discern because desiring for the ministry footprint of a church to increase certainly has biblical support. But when the definition of "growth" is limited only to narrow metrics like "how many people showed up for worship?" or "how much money is landing in the offering plate?" we are straying from the mission Jesus is calling us to.

- A desire and culture of deliberately focusing on NOT being like other churches. During an onsite consulting visit with a church, I suspected that they were being guided by an unhealthy motive. To validate or eliminate my suspicion, I asked the lead pastor to describe the purpose of the church in one sentence. His answer was telling. "We are not Saddleback." As I probed further, it became clear to me that the church primarily existed as a declaration that the ministry approach of Saddleback Church was wrong. Sadly, instead of reflecting on the dysfunction of this approach, the church remained true to its stated purpose, disintegrated into dysfunction, and closed its doors a few months later.

- The desire to be on the cutting edge. Some church leaders run from conference to conference (more recently from webinar to webinar) looking for the next best thing to do. Frequently, without prayer or contextual reflection, they quickly put into practice the latest "best practice" they picked up from the latest conference experience. Being a part of one of these churches feels a little bit like riding on a roller coaster.

Motives rooted in scripture are far more stable and will have long-lasting positive impacts. Some examples of scriptural principles that can serve as the biblical guardrails for a reimagination process may include the narrative about the earliest church from Acts 2 or Peter's metaphor for the Church in 1 Peter 2.

Step Three – A Guiding Framework

Listening prayer invites God to do what only He can do. Shaping the dream that God is birthing in our hearts into a picture of the summit that we can see together is our responsibility. A well-developed guiding framework will help us sort out which peak we aim for. Making the vision tangible is as much about deciding what we won't do as it is about what we will do.

Increasingly, leaders are finding that the Twelve Shifts framework described in the book *Next Wave* is a helpful tool for zeroing in on a preferred future. Here are some thoughts about how the framework can help you and your team in the process of reimagination. This framework will give you traction and clarity around what destination you truly want to pursue—and what destinations you don't!

The Twelve Shifts

Shift One

Rediscover the Church—from building the institution to catalyzing a movement

In the reimagined church, the sign that the Church is present will be the tangible existence of a community of disciples with Jesus on His Mission.

Shift Two

Reimagine Discipleship—from discipleship as a program to a lifestyle of disciple-making

In the reimagined church, the primary action of the church will be that disciples are being made by church members as they go.

Shift Three

Reinvent Funding—from self-sustaining to sustainable

The economic strategies of the reimagined church will no longer be limited to tithes and offerings as the primary source of operating funds.

Shift Four

Rethink Team-Building—from titles and positions to communities of disciples on mission with Jesus.

The foundational team members of the reimagined church will themselves be practicing disciple-makers first and then ministry specialists.

Shift Five

Redeem Architecture—from empty buildings to fully utilized assets

The reimagined church will view property as an asset to be used to further the mission of Jesus rather than a sacred space reserved only for holy activities.

Shift Six

Reclaim the Ecosystem—from isolating to complementing

The reimagined church will connect broadly and creatively with a diversity of organizations and entities that together make up the ecosystem of the community they serve.

Shift Seven

Recalibrate the Timeline—from launching to emerging

The reimagined church will embrace the long obedience process of becoming rather than the temptation of a quick-fix approach.

Shift Eight

Refresh the Metrics—from bodies in the pews to disciples in the marketplace

The reimagined church will discover new tangible ways to measure missional progress that connect celebration to being faithful to the mission of Jesus.

Shift Nine

Refocus Church Habits—from calendar-driven to mission-driven

The reimagined church will find the right ministry rhythm for the specific context in which they serve.

Shift Ten

Reconsider Core Values—from institution-focused to mission-oriented

The reimagined church will be motivated by values that are meticulously aligned with the mission of Jesus.

Shift Eleven

Recommit to Multiplication—from addition to movement

The reimagined church will not be content with a framework of addition but will intentionally organize around frameworks that encourage missional multiplication that leads to a self-sustaining movement.

Shift Twelve

Reactivate Spirit Dependency—from duty to necessity

The reimagined church will avoid simply mimicking the ministry strategies of others but, instead, be rigorously dependent on the guidance of the Spirit to find their way forward.

Notice that the Twelve Shifts framework above does not provide a prescriptive picture of what the reimagined church should look like. That is very intentional. The last thing the Church needs to do is find a cookie-cutter approach to being the church in every context. As you embrace this season of reimagining the church—we suspect that the already emerging vision of the future church being birthed in your heart will increasingly align with the principles contained in this framework.

Step Four – A Commitment to See the Process Through

On May 25, 1961, President John F. Kennedy announced the goal of safely sending an American to the moon before the end of the decade. Almost exactly eight years later, that goal was achieved on July 20, 1969. Those intervening eight years were filled with triumphs, protests, amazing discoveries, and tragic setbacks that no one could have foreseen when President Kennedy shared the goal. But he and the incredible NASA team— cheered on by most, but not all, of the country—pressed tenaciously forward to see the dream come true. Standing on the moon would not have become a reality without a sincere commitment to see the process through.

In the next chapter, we will be thinking together about something author Jeanie Duck calls "The Change Monster."[7] Her basic premise is

---

7   Jeanie Daniel Duck, _The Change Monster,_ (New York, NY: Crown Business Books, 2001).

that most change efforts are sabotaged in the earliest stages because of predictable obstacles that tend to plague every change effort. A successful reimagining process requires a relentless commitment to push through the inevitable obstructions and setbacks you will encounter. Tenacity, grit, and a long obedience in the same direction must be embodied for a reimagine process to be effective.

When you say "yes" to a destination, you must be willing to say "no" to everything else.

Reimagination processes are commonly derailed by sideways energy. Effectively reimagining the church will mean staying true to the direction that God has called you to. This means you must be prepared to say no to everything else. The collective vision of the destination must be clear enough in the minds and hearts of the reimagine team that every individual can recognize and steer clear of an emerging option that does not fit.

Step Five – Agreement on a Compelling Destination

You've practiced listening prayer, identified your scripture-based motivations, filtered your vision through a guiding framework, and committed to the process. Now it's time to find clarity and agreement in how the end result will look.

Here are some guidelines for making the destination clear and unifying.

- **The destination must capture the imagination.**

  In 2004, Steve Jobs had something in mind that no one had ever seen before—the iPhone. And he had a huge challenge—everyone was content with their state-of-the-art flip phones. All the cool kids were using their Blackberries to stay one step ahead of the competition. Blackberry became the envy of the mobile phone industry by incrementally improving their phone a little bit every year. How do you get everyone to pivot from their Blackberries to an unproven something they had never seen before? It seemed like an impossible assignment.

Effectively leading a reimagination process begins with the same challenge. How do you help a content group of Christ followers to pivot from their known way of being the Church to an unproven something they've never seen before?

Steve Jobs overcame his challenge by demonstrating a new phone that was completely different and so dramatically superior to the phone that everyone currently held in their hands. Wise reimagination leaders will help their faith communities form a compelling, attractive, and Jesus-centered vision of the Church that motivates them to trade in their flip phones for something better—way better.

For leaders in the church that Jesus is building, seeing the destination clearly begins with letting go of what you think you know. Your destination is not an incremental improvement on your favorite flip phone. The needed destination is something new birthed out of God's heart. Knowing God's heart means connecting with Him in prayer, solitude, and a posture of listening. Carefully discerning the dream in God's heart will lead you toward a destination that will capture the imagination of those who are called to take the journey with you.

· Everyone must agree on the destination.

This is more difficult than it sounds. If you've been a church leader for more than one day, you've already learned that people smiling at you and nodding their heads in agreement do not necessarily mean they are on the same page with you. Apparent agreement means nothing if their actions remain the same. You will know who sees the destination by what they do. Verbal agreement and heads nodding in affirmation will not suffice.

- ### Reimagining a church will only happen if behaviors and habits change.

Verbal agreement and heads nodding in affirmation will not suffice. Changed habits and behaviors moving in the same direction are the surest signs of agreement about the destination.

- ### The reimagine destination is different than restarting and relaunching.

As you envision the reimagine process, it's important to keep this principle clear: restarting is simply resuming the exact same things you've done in the past. Relaunching resembles incremental improvements on a Blackberry. Reimagining starts from scratch. Nothing from the past is brought forward unless it is deemed essential for the new vision of the future.

- ### Reimagination is like nothing you've ever seen before.

To guide people there, you've got to all be seeing the same thing.

This is truly the greatest challenge of the reimagination journey. You are leading people toward a future that you've never seen yourself! You are discovering it together as you follow the Spirit. You will have moments of uncertainty, and yet collectively, the community will have a sense of confidence that they are faithfully on mission with Jesus. The tension this ambiguity creates will challenge every leadership bone in your body.

You may be feeling a little frustrated right now because you wanted this book to tell you what the twenty-first-century destination looks like. If you need a paint-by-numbers approach to shaping the church, then reimagining the church is not for you. Plenty of resources are available to help you lead a church that will effectively reach twentieth-century culture. That is not a bad thing. Plenty of places are still heavily influenced by a twentieth-century mindset. Healthy churches are needed in those places too.

Reimagining is about transitioning the church you lead to something you've never seen before that will enable the church to make tangible missional progress. This book will not hand you a blueprint for what your church should look like going forward. You can—and will—thank me later.

Putting It All Together

If you've ever watched the Kentucky Derby, you know that the race itself is the end of a long process. The horses that end up in the race are carefully bred from champion parents. They arrive at the racetrack days before the race occurs. In the hours preceding the call to post, the horses, their handlers, and their jockeys go through the same exact process in the same exact order, every year. Years, months, days, and hours go by before the gates open and the race begins.

The reimagine process will require some careful preparation just to get you to the starting point. It's not a process to be casually entered into on a whim. Starting with the end in mind involves listening prayer, scripture-based motivation, a guiding framework, a commitment to see the process through, and a clear vision of the destination. All of these elements need to be in place before you begin the process.

Here's a graphic representation of what beginning with the end in mind looks like.

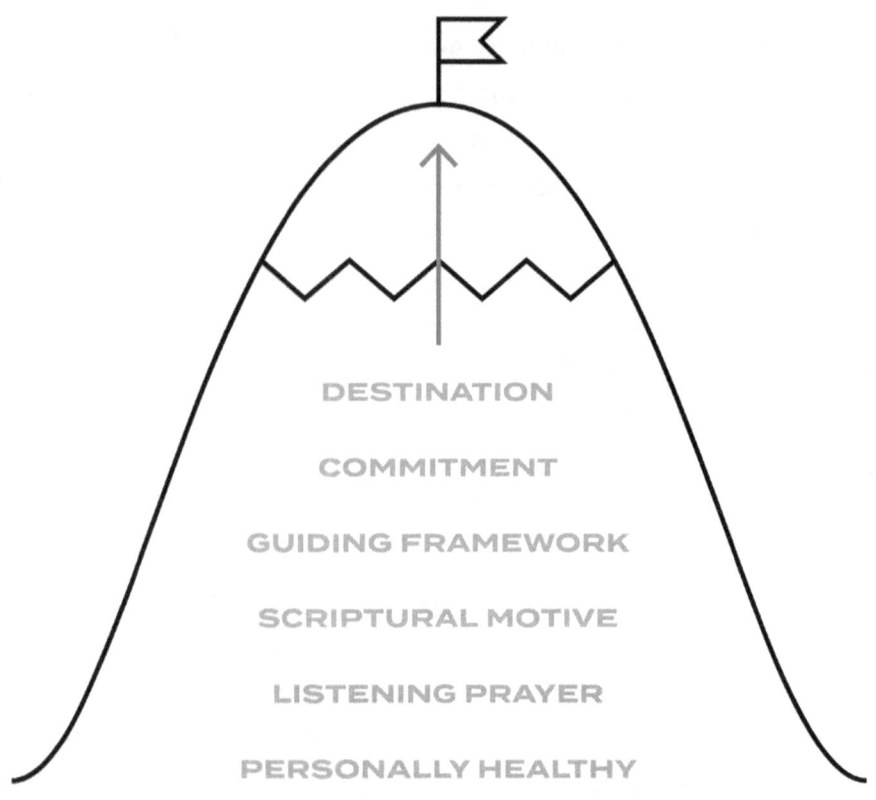

DESTINATION

COMMITMENT

GUIDING FRAMEWORK

SCRIPTURAL MOTIVE

LISTENING PRAYER

PERSONALLY HEALTHY

Before you begin putting one foot in front of the other, it will be helpful to look at the reimagination process through one more preparatory lens: the "Lifecycle Lens." That will be the subject of our next chapter.

Beginning with the end in mind is an essential step in your "get ready" process. In the Next Wave Community, learn more ways you can get ready for twenty-first-century ministry. Join the Next Wave Community today using the QR code below.

CHAPTER THREE

LIFECYCLE

Understanding Your Personal and Organizational Lifecycle

The Parable of Pastor Pat

For the first time in his ministry journey, Pat had decided to get away to unplug from the grind and really, really listen for the voice of Jesus. He chose to spend a week at a retreat in the mountains designed specifically for that purpose. No cell signal. No Wi-Fi. No televisions, radios or any other form of contact with the outside world. He was alone with his thoughts and a hunger to hear God's voice. At first, the quiet and lack of demands to attend to was almost disturbing. But by the third day, he began to hear God whispering in his heart. He wrote down what he was hearing. A picture of the reimagined church began to form in his mind.

Pat returned from his personal retreat feeling a tiny tinge of hope wriggling around in his heart. He felt energized by the vision that God was birthing in him. He could imagine the incredible positive impact that forming new missional habits would make in the lives of his church members and in the hearts of people who still needed to hear and see the Gospel

lived out in real life. He talked it over with his wife. "I think
I'm ready for this, but what about this church? Are they ready?
What is this effort going to require of them? Are they willing
to give it?" His wife, Jordan, was usually straightforward
with him, and this time was no exception. "Those are really
important questions," she replied. "Before you take any more
steps toward this reimagination process, it will be smart for
you to do your homework. Even if you are up for the challenge,
you might be signing up for a suicide mission. I don't want to
see us go through that."

Pregnancy. Birth. Infancy. Childhood. The teen years. Young
adulthood leads to middle age. The senior years are followed by hospice
care and death. Sound familiar? All of us pass through these stages of life.
Each stage has some universal elements shared by every living person.
At the same time, every stage is contextually unique for each individual.
Everyone reading these words has traversed through the "birth" phase.
But some of us were born in hospitals, some in the car on the way
to the hospital, and others were born at home. Once born, all of us
become infants, then toddlers, and then children—in that order. Yet
our experience in each of those phases of life is distinctive from the lived
experience of everyone else.

So it is with a local church. Every church has a lifecycle. At some
point, a local church is birthed, grows, matures, plateaus, declines, and
one day, it will cease to exist. Why does this matter for our discussion
of reimagining a church? Because the reimagining process will be greatly
impacted by what season the church is in on its lifecycle spectrum.

Setting out to reimagine a church without understanding its place on
the lifecycle spectrum is to sabotage the process before it even begins.

In this chapter, you will learn to diagnose the location of your church on the lifecycle spectrum and understand how the lifecycle position will impact the reimagination process. Let's begin with an overview of the normal lifecycle of the average church.

Lifecycle Overview

Social scientists who study organizational lifecycle development have created a conceptual tool called the "Sigmoidal Curve" to help leaders understand the normal lifecycle expectancies of organizations (including churches). "The Sigmoidal Curve is a mathematical concept used to model the natural lifecycle of many things from biological organisms to schools, churches, companies, marriages, and careers."[8]

The curve is basically a deformed letter "S" lying on its side.

THE SIGMOIDAL CURVE

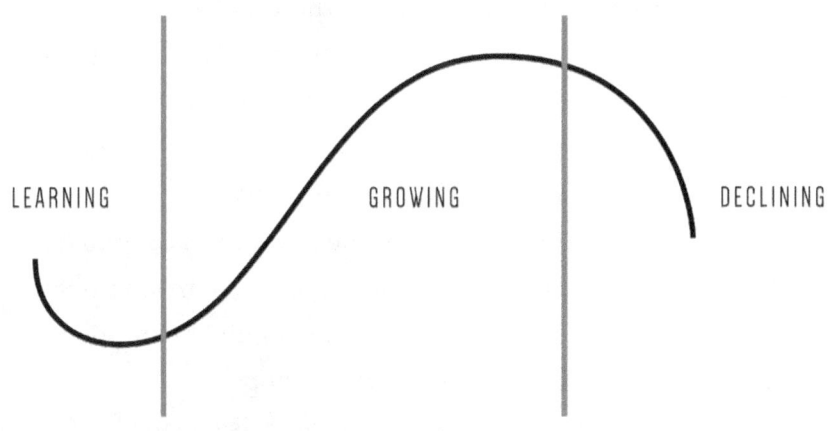

LEARNING   GROWING   DECLINING

---

8   Dumb Little Man Website, "The Lesson of the Sigmoidal Curve," accessed on March 1, 2024. https://www.dumblittleman.com/lesson-of-sigmoid-curve/

The Sigmoidal Curve illustrates the three basic phases of the lifecycle of organisms and organizations:

During the "**Learning**" phase, the organism or organization is discovering how to thrive (or not) in the context into which it is emerging. The downslope of the learning phase represents the challenges and obstacles that must be overcome for the organism/organization to enter into the "Growing" phase of the lifecycle. During the **"Growing"** phase, the organism/organization has discovered the necessary skills and found the right momentum to enter into a time of optimistic growth and prosperity. Inevitably (without intervention), the organism/organization enters into the **"Declining"** phase when it loses the ability to thrive, and eventually the organism/organization will cease to exist.

Note that the curve represents quality of missional effectiveness more than quantity. This means that during the learning phase, the downward slant of the curve represents frustration and uncertainty about the ability of the organism/organization to thrive. The upward and then flattening shape of the "Growing" phase represents the positive progress toward mission and the arrival at a state of equilibrium where the organization is most effective with the least amount of effort. The downward slope of the "Declining" phase represents the general inability of the organization to recapture the "glory days" of the "Growing" phase.

The dominant emotion of the Learning phase can be summarized as hopeful frustration. The dominant emotion of the Growing phase can be summarized as optimistic excitement. The dominant emotion of the Declining phase can be summarized as fading hope.

Remember, the path of the Sigmoidal Curve is inevitable. But note that we added in parenthesis "without intervention." That means this curve is incredibly prophetic about the destiny of an organization if it simply follows the path of least resistance. If you've ever been part of the startup of a church, you may remember the heady days at the very beginning. The catalyst team gathered and dreamed together about what the new church was going to be. The catalyst team buys into a common vision that unifies and energizes them through the startup challenges. In the illustration below, we've placed an "X" on the Sigmoidal Curve where the achievement of the unifying vision occurs. The catalyst team agrees on the "X" and then sets out to make it a reality.

THE VISION
REALIZED

The team collectively presses through the hard early days when it feels like the vision is getting further away instead of nearer. But then the tide turns and the church begins to move toward the shared vision. Excitement and optimism reign. Everyone is working hard, but everyone can see that progress is happening, so they press on. Finally, the day comes when the vision is a reality. Everyone can see it. Everyone knows it.

I remember when that day arrived during my first church plant. From the beginning, my vision for the church was tied to a number. A church planting expert told me that for the church to be a long-term success, we needed to grow to 200 people quickly. He was wrong, but that's a discussion for another book! But at the time, his words played in the back of my mind like a broken record. Our vision was to grow to be a church of 200 as quickly as possible. "A church of 200" meant at least 200 people gathering weekly for worship. Everything we did was about that number. And the day came when the head usher handed me a little piece of paper similar to the one he handed me every week. It was the "how many noses and how many nickels" report. I don't remember the "nickels" number, but the "noses" number was 205! Wow! There it was in black and white. The number we had been working so hard to see. 200. In fact, it was more than 200. I felt a surge of excitement, accomplishment, and, in all honesty—some pride. But I felt something else. A sense of relief. A sense that we had arrived. A sense that, for the first time in a long time, we could relax and enjoy our achievements.

This story is a snapshot of what arriving at the "X" looks like for an organization. That sense of "we have arrived" leads to the next segment of the Sigmoidal Curve for the organization—the plateau at the end of the growth phase. The plateau is tricky because it feels kind of like the church is running on cruise control. The classes are staffed. The small groups are meeting. The worship services are acceptably full. The catalyst team is grateful to be enjoying the fruits of their sacrifice and labor. A critical mass has been achieved that allows the church to experience a sense of accomplishment and stability at the same time. It's normal for the flat part of the "Growing" phase to last for a long time—months, years, and even decades, which is all fine and good but very deceptive. Because something is missing, which will inevitably lead to the day when the curve points downward into the "declining" phase of the lifecycle curve.

That's why the day a church arrives at the "X" is the most dangerous day in the life of the church. The day I received the news that 205 people had showed up for worship felt like a victory, but it could have also been the beginning of the end. We'd been working hard for years to achieve that goal. Our team was celebrating but tired. I was tired. I felt a sense of relief and was grateful that we could relax now that we had achieved our goal. Thankfully, the Holy Spirit interrupted my victory celebration with a very powerful set of questions. "How many showed up for worship today?" He whispered. "205," I proudly responded. "How many didn't show up for worship today?" He asked. "Uhhh. Oh my." I exclaimed. And just like that, I was reminded of the number that mattered to God. About 200,000 people lived within thirty minutes of our worship space.

I was reminded of a story Jesus told that directly confronted my obsession with the "how many showed up" question.

> *Then Jesus told them this parable: "Suppose one of you has a hundred sheep and loses one of them. Doesn't he leave the ninety-nine in the open country and go after the lost sheep until he finds it? And when he finds it, he joyfully puts it on his shoulders and goes home. Then he calls his friends and neighbors together and says, 'Rejoice with me; I have found my lost sheep.' I tell you that in the same way there will be more rejoicing in heaven over one sinner who repents than over ninety-nine righteous persons who do not need to repent.*[9]

My fixation with reaching 200 participants had caused me to lose sight of the bigger mission to which we were called. It was indeed good that 200 had shown up to worship Jesus, but the gentle prompting of the Holy Spirit reminded me that we were just getting started. I quickly realized that the next phase of the journey would require a new, compelling vision. No one would blame us if we just put on cruise

---

9   Luke 15:3-7 NIV

control and lived life as a good, faithful church of 200. That put us in the top 10 percent of churches in Utah as measured by Sunday attendance. We were "better than average." But if we wanted to vigorously pursue being with Jesus on His Mission, we needed to see our current reality as a starting point toward a new vision. We needed to intentionally start a new curve.

That's what we mean by intervention. The Sigmoidal Curve concept predicts that it is normal for an organism/organization to generally follow the path of the Sigmoidal Curve. This means that churches will inevitably end up on the downward slide of the "Declining" phase. Indeed, this appears to be the plight of most North American churches. They are born, they live and even thrive for a while, but then, inevitably, they decline and die. The way to tell a different story than the inevitable path of the Sigmoidal Curve is to discover God's next vision for the church and set in motion a new curve.

Authors Nicholas Imparato and Oren Harari call this "Jumping the Curve."[10] Their book by that name is a classic text for business leaders seeking to navigate the challenges and opportunities of the unstable days in which we live. The "jumping the curve" concept may have been written by business leaders for business applications, but the principles communicated are timeless and clearly applicable to leaders seeking to lead a church through a process of reimagination. The authors suggest that to break the cycle of inevitability, it is necessary to intentionally "jump the curve."

Intentional intervention is what they mean by "jumping the curve." For organizational leaders, it means starting a new curve—*on purpose.*

---

10   Nicholas Imparato and Oren Harari, Jossey-Bass , *Jumping the Curve* (San Fransisco, CA: Jossey-Bass, Inc., 1994).

On the Sigmoidal Curve, the ideal time to start a new curve is just before the achievement of the first vision. This timing allows the organization to capitalize on the momentum of the efforts to achieve the first vision point. The current vision is celebrated and the new vision is cast.

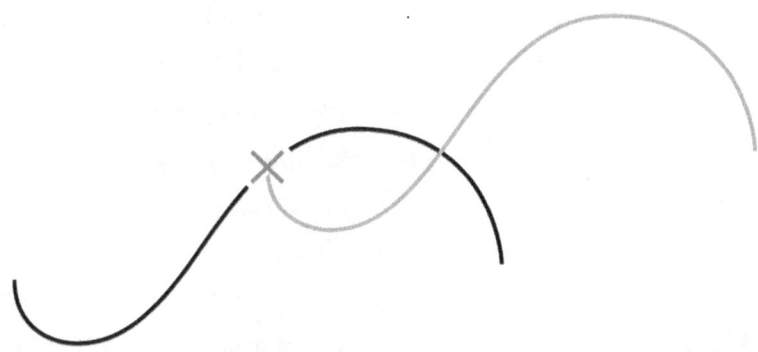

Ideally, thriving organizations will jump the curve over and over again, as illustrated below.

**LIFE CYCLE OF A
LONG-LIVED ORGANIZATION**

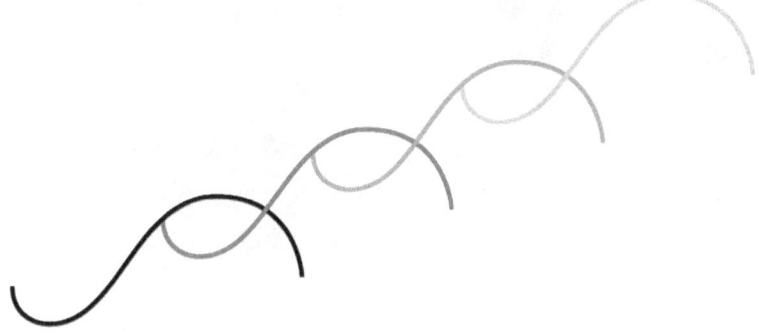

The Sigmoidal Curve is a crucial tool for understanding the reimagining readiness of the church you lead. The first step is to plot where the church is on the Lifecycle Curve. You've probably already done that in your head, but take a moment right now to draw a curve on a paper or tablet and then put an "X" that represents the place of church on the curve. Better yet, pull team members together, explain the curve concept, and then ask them to independently plot where they think the church is on the curve. Then ask everyone to explain their reason for placing the "X" where they did. This is a simple way to gauge the unity—or lack thereof—of your team with the current state of the church. It will also serve as a helpful catalyst for a rich team conversation until you reach a consensus on where the church's "X" should be placed on the curve. Hang on to that thought—we'll come back to it in a minute.

Understanding the Change Monster

By now, you recognize that the reimagination process is a form of jumping the curve. When you jump the curve, you start a completely new curve, which means that no matter where your church is, you are deliberately choosing to go back to the beginning. It is essential to understand what it means to "begin a new curve." Underestimating the challenges of starting a new curve will likely doom you to failure.

In her book *The Change Monster*,[11] Jeanie Daniel Duck has provided a fantastic planning tool for navigating the process of starting a new curve. She notes that most depictions of the Sigmoidal Curve start with the curve going down before it goes up. The reason for the downslope is what she calls "The Change Monster." Her book zooms in on the nuances

---

11   Jeanie Daniel Duck, *The Change Monster* (New York, NY: Crown Business Books, 2001), pgs. 16-17.

of the earliest steps of starting a new curve. Many leaders have found her insight both helpful and prophetic. Wise leaders will factor them in when considering the cost of stepping into a process of reimagination.

Following is a blow up of the initial phase of the Sigmoidal Curve.

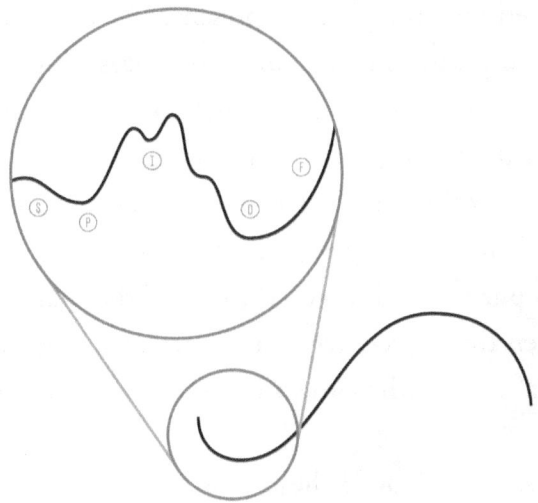

A new Sigmoidal Curve begins with a decision to change because the present state of stagnation (indicated in the diagram by the circled letter "S") has become unacceptable to a critical mass of the congregation. The leaders then engage in a time of planning and strategy formation, represented by the circled letter "P" in the diagram. P= planning/strategy—during this phase, the picture of the preferred future is clarified and tangible action steps are formed. These actions steps are intended to get us from where we are to the preferred future. The "P" phase is mostly optimistic because real action steps are about to be set in motion. However, at this point, everything is theoretical, so the plans have not yet run into the meat grinder of reality. Once plans are made, the church enters into a period of Implementation, represented by the circled letter "I" in the diagram. Here's where the Change Monster really begins to make itself known. Most leaders expect everything to be "up and to the right" once the implementation phase is happening.

But Duck suggests that it is normal for a change process to pass through a "Determination" phase (represented by a circled letter "D" in the diagram) and push through some sort of crisis, ultimately arriving at a point where the change is either abandoned or results begin to be realized. "D" is the meat grinder of reality. Opposition, unanticipated challenges, people acting in their own best interest, etc.—all of these conspire to challenge the implementation of the best-laid plans. Some have called this phase the "death of a vision." If the change process is not abandoned, then the church begins to experience the "Fruition" phase of the Sigmoidal Curve, where the original vision begins to tangibly take shape.

The leadership concept of the Change Monster is a tried-and-true reality that impacts every change effort regardless of the nature of the organization. Ignore it at your own peril or embrace it and prepare for the ride. Anticipating the bumpy nature of starting a new curve increases the probability that you will see the curve through to the fruition of the vision.

Keeping the mission and destination always in front of you while going through the bumps and potholes of the Change Monster is crucial. You will experience discouragement and the temptation to revert back to what you know during this phase. Keeping the mission and destination at the forefront will help you stay focused during this long transitional phase.

"When we planted our church, God had given us an unexpected vision to "pastor the community," but we did not understand what that could look like—so we did what we knew how to do. We gathered a small team and began holding services that looked like every other church around us. We were focused on the traditional Sunday morning experience and not on what it meant to "pastor a community." While serving as a chaplain for our local police department, I saw a need in our community that was being overlooked. In our suburban setting, there were pockets of families living in extended-stay hotels that were struggling and overlooked. Through a series of events and partnerships, we begin to serve the families living in these extended-stay hotels. As we began to put more and more time and effort into serving the needs of this overlooked community, many of the families that were originally part of the church plant began to leave. It was very discouraging, but we held on to this vision to "pastor a community." We sought out new partnerships within the community and planned our calendar around this unreached community. Now six years later, we are seeing the fruit of the work that we are called to, and our influence in the community continues to grow."

—Larry Grawey

Looking at Your Life through the Lifecycle Lens

Here's a worthwhile question—where are you on your personal Sigmoidal Curve? Just getting started? Feeling velocity? Enjoying the fruits of your vision? Ready to give up? Or are you on your third or fourth curve, preparing to jump another one? Pause and reflect on where you are currently because the answer will help you know your personal readiness to lead your church through a reimagination process. Take a moment to plot your "X" on your personal lifecycle curve.

The Leadership Stage Index

The Leadership Stage Index is a guideline that helps leaders understand how they are viewed by the congregation over time. This simple tool is an extremely relevant reference point for anyone desiring to lead a church through the reimagining process. The Leadership Stage Index proposes three stages of perceived leadership status. When a new leader is selected to lead a congregation, for the first three years, they are viewed as a chaplain. As chaplains, they are expected to preach great sermons, visit people in the hospital, and make sure the church budget is well-managed. After three years, if they serve well as a chaplain, they may be accepted as the pastor. As a pastor, they are respected for their spiritual stewardship of the church. They are viewed as reliable spiritual guides and trusted to cultivate the spiritual well-being of the members of the church.

If they serve well in the pastor role for another three years, they may be perceived as the "leader." As a leader, their voice has become the trusted guide for decisions about the future of the church. They are now viewed with respect when they introduce new ideas and cast vision for the church's next season. At the "leader" stage of the leadership stage index, the leader is optimally positioned to lead the church through significant change processes (building programs, reimagination, ministry style adjustments, etc.).

Observations about the Leadership Stage Index

1. The index provides a general rule of thumb that should be factored into decisions about the timing of a reimagination

process. If you have just recently arrived at the church you lead, you need to be cautious about challenging the entire church to step into a radical transformation process. They need time to learn to trust you as a leader.

2. A quick overview of the research around pastoral longevity puts the average pastoral tenure at about four years. This means that about 50 percent of pastors stay just long enough to be viewed as spiritual guides but leave before they are viewed as the leader.

3. The length of each phase is determined by many factors, but every leader will pass through each phase. One factor that determines the length of each phase is the governance style of the church. If a church is led by appointed leaders, the phases tend to last longer. If a church is led by elected leaders, the phases tend to be shorter. Another significant factor in the phase length is the history of the church. If the church has had a series of short-term pastors, the phases will tend to be longer. On the other hand, if the church has been blessed with long-term, healthy pastors, the phases may tend to be shorter.

4. One of the great advantages of being a church planter is that you are the leader from day one. The six- to seven-year runway does not apply.

Let the reader be aware! If you are the newly elected/appointed pastor of the church you lead, you should be very cautious about leading the church into a reimagination process. Your good intentions will not overcome a lack of trust or confidence in your leadership. Trust and confidence take time to develop.

How to Determine Reimagination Readiness

Jesus once said: "For which of you, desiring to build a tower, does not first sit down and count the cost, whether he has enough to complete it? Otherwise, when he has laid a foundation and is not able to finish, all who see it begin to mock him, saying, 'This man began to build and was not able to finish'"(Luke 14:28-30).

The Reimagine Readiness Assessment Tool

Entering into a reimagination process is a cost that should be counted. In the "Get Ready" segment of this book, we've shared some of the factors that need to be considered in the count. Here are some diagnostic questions that will help you assess your readiness for leading a reimagination process.

1. What is your personal health level? Give yourself a number on a scale of 1–10 (1 being very unhealthy, 10 being very healthy.)

2. How much clarity do you have regarding the reimagine destination? Give your clarity a number on a scale of 1–10 (1 being very fuzzy and hard to put into words, 10 being very clear and easily communicated.)

3. Where is the church on the lifecycle curve? Assign a number from 1–10 (1 being in sharp decline, 5 being in the learning phase, 10 being in the growing phase)

4. Where are you personally on the lifecycle curve? Assign a number from 1–10 (1 being tired and ready to retire, 5 being new in your role, 10 being an established leader, full of energy)

5. Where are you on the Leadership Phase Index? Assign a number from 1–10 (1 being a brand new "chaplain," 5 being in the

"pastor" phase, 10 being a trusted leader with a strong track record and solid group of followers.)

Factor	Assessed Score
Personal Health	
Destination Clarity	
Church Lifecycle Curve	
Personal Lifecycle Curve	
Leadership Phase Index	
Total	

Add up your numbers. If the total is 0–20, now is not a good time for you to step into the journey of leading a reimagine process. If your total is 21–35, a caution flag is vigorously waving. A reimagination process may be ill-advised at this time. If your total is 36–50, you may have a green light to step out and lead a reimagine process.

If the light is green, it's time to move from the "Get Ready" phase to the "Get Set" phase of the reimagine journey. Getting set is all about determining who will lead with you on this journey. Identifying the reimagine guiding coalition will be the subject of the next several chapters.

Join the Next Wave Community today using the QR code below to learn how other leaders determined their readiness for the reimagine process.

PART TWO

GET SET

CONGRATULATIONS!

You've made it to the starting line of the reimagining process. You've paused to thoughtfully take account of your personal health, the clarity of your destination, the church lifecycle curve, your personal lifecycle curve, and your leadership phase index. You've received at least a high yellow in your reimagining readiness assessment.

It's time to make the big announcement to the entire church!

NOT!

We've still got work to do. It's time to get set. The next few chapters will help you prepare your heart and mind for the implementation of the reimagination process.

CHAPTER FOUR

EXPECT
Not Everyone Can Make the Switch

The Parable of Pastor Pat

Pat's assessment score on the "Reimagine Readiness Index" was a solid 33. Not necessarily a full-blown green light, but not a red light either. Closer to green than red. So, Pat thought, "Let's Go!"

The process of working through the Readiness Index tool had helped Pat recognize some of the potential land mines and challenges he would face as he led the church through the reimagination process. He felt cautiously confident that he was the right leader to help the church find its way forward into a thriving ministry future. He was aware that the church had been stuck in neutral for a long time, so expecting a quick turnaround was unrealistic. But he'd been at the church long enough to have earned trust and buy-in from the key influencers.

The biggest concern he had was a reality that every change leader faces. People don't like change. He could see no way around the default posture of resistance to change. Resistance to change can only be managed. Yeah, but how?

THIS CHAPTER FOCUSES ON THIS hard, cold truth—nobody likes change. Nobody. Here are some actual quotes that illustrate the built-in resistance to change that is hardwired into being human.

"There's no chance that the iPhone is going to get any significant market share."
> –Steve Ballmer, Microsoft CEO, 2007

"Television won't be able to hold on to any market it captures after the first six months. People will soon get tired of staring at a plywood box every night."
> –Darryl Zanuck, executive at Twentieth Century Fox, 1946

"The horse is here to stay, but the automobile is only a novelty—a fad."
> –President of the Michigan Savings Bank advising Henry Ford's lawyer, Horace Rackham, not to invest in the Ford Motor Company, 1903

"The Americans have need of the telephone, but we do not. We have plenty of messenger boys."
> –Sir William Preece, Chief Engineer, British Post Office, 1876

As illustrated by the quotes above, even very smart people don't like to change. If a person tells you they like change, they are probably being dishonest.

In fact, most people would rather die than change. In an article in *Fast Company*, "Change or Die," Author Alan Deutschman shares the startling results of a comprehensive scientific study on willingness to change.

Writing about the behaviors of patients recovering from coronary bypass surgery, Deutschman observes. "…many patients could avoid the return of pain and the need to repeat the surgery—not to mention arrest the course of their disease before it kills them—by switching to healthier lifestyles. Yet very few do." He goes on to quote Dr. Edward Miller, dean of the medical school and CEO of Johns Hopkins Hospital. "If you look at people after coronary-artery bypass grafting two years later, 90 percent of them have not changed their lifestyle," Miller said. "And that's been studied over and over and over again. And so we're missing a link in there. Even though they know they have a very bad disease, and they know they should change their lifestyle, for whatever reason, they can't." [12]

People would literally rather die than change.

This inborn resistance to change increases exponentially in a church. Perhaps due to the constantly shifting changes happening all the time in the general culture, churches are viewed as a refuge from chaos, a peaceful garden where one can escape to find calm. Over time, church folks settle into the comfortable rhythm of the same music style, preaching style, and even where they prefer to sit.

Layer on top of this innate reluctance to change the misguided theological idea that Jesus never changes (that part is true) and neither should we (that's the misguided part). The result is that efforts to alter the rhythm of the church are viewed as dangerous and probably heretical.

This is why the default position of many churches is resistance to change and the underlying belief that any change effort represents a threat to God's perfect will.

Here's another fact that must be considered in this equation—most spiritual leaders overestimate the persuasive power of their words to

12   Fast Company Website, "Change or Die," article by Alan Deutschman, May 1, 2005 edition of Fast Company.

inspire change. Rookie leaders (and way too many veterans) mistakenly think they have the ability to conjure up the right mix of words and emotions to lead their congregation through a 180-degree course correction in one powerful sermon or, at the most, a series of sermons.

The idea that a reimagine process can happen quickly and everyone in the church will be thrilled with it is as factual as the tooth fairy. It's a fantasy that has no chance of becoming a reality.

The good news is that a reimagining process CAN happen in your church if you are willing to work through a deliberate process of leading change that factors in the hard truths that people don't like to change and leaders don't like to wait.

To successfully lead a change process, you must wisely manage your expectations.

Here are some expectations about people that must be significantly changed in order to successfully lead a church through a reimagine process.

Expectation: Everyone will happily change.

Truth: Most people will be resistant to change.

Expectation: Everyone will joyfully participate in the change process.

Truth: Many will not.

Expectation: After the reimagine process, all of the current members will still be part of the church and new ones will have been added.

Truth: Not everyone who is part of the church before the reimagination process will be with you when the reimagination process is complete.

Getting your expectations in the right place is good, but it will not solve the fundamental challenge—if most people are resistant to change, then how do I talk them into changing?

The answer? Wait for it.

Don't.

Don't expect them to change, don't ask them to change, don't be disappointed in them if they don't change. Don't try to change them. Don't allow yourself to think of them as dumb, stuck, or uninformed. Some of them will be exceptionally smart people. Resist the temptation to set up an either/or scenario—" either you embrace the change I'm promoting, or you are on the wrong side of history."

Wise leaders understand it's all about both/and. Throw out "my way or the highway" thinking. That will sabotage your ability to lead change. Embrace the "both/and." Resist the temptation to ask a bunch of people who are happily set in their ways to throw it all out and act completely differently. That. Will. Not. Happen.

Both/and means this: Leave everything the same and start something new. How to do that will be the primary focus of this book. But for now, you only need to know you don't and won't need to change everybody in the church. Seriously. Lay that aspiration aside. Why? Because if you don't, you'll never be able to lead the church successfully through the process of reimagination.

Why do I keep repeating myself?

Because upon hearing this counsel, many well-intended church leaders decide they are the exception to the rule and try to bring everyone along anyway. I know this because I've been there and done that. Here are some reasons we (church leaders) are so optimistic about our ability to lead change.

1. We genuinely love people, and we don't want to see anyone left behind.

2. We are confident that they will thank us when the changes are fully in place because everyone will be so much better off.

3. We find it hard to believe that everyone can't see the benefits of the new path as clearly as we do. We are sure that if we explain it, pump it, show it, and share it enough, everyone will eventually come around.

4. We are convinced that unity demands that everyone move forward together in lockstep.

For all of the above reasons and more, church leaders often choose to fight against one of the most immutable characteristics of human nature—people don't naturally embrace change. We keep thinking we are the ones who will pull it off. We will bring everyone with us through the reimagination process. Thinking like this sets us up for deep and painful disappointment, not to mention emotionally stressful partings of the way with friends we love dearly.

We need a better strategy than denial. Let's replace "denying the inevitable" with "embracing the fact" that by choosing to embark on a process of reimagination, we will inevitably need to part ways with people we genuinely love. Some will jump ship almost immediately. Others will leave slowly, perhaps prolonging the agony for you and for them. Going separate ways will happen, so let's do it well. Here are some guidelines for skillfully parting ways.

1. **Choose to let them go with grace.** You want to believe that the best thing for them is to stay and benefit from the changes you are leading the church into. The truth is, most of the time, it's best for people who are resistant to change to find another

worshiping community where they want to belong. You can serve them well by helping them find the place they need to go.

2. **Make it easy for them to come back**. Avoid the temptation to alienate the people who are choosing to leave. Instead, let them know that they will always be welcome to return to the church.

3. **Never speak negatively about those who leave.** Even if people leave "loudly," publicly complaining and criticizing you and your leaders, do not return fire with fire. Do not allow yourself to be pulled into a cycle of blame and character assassination. Do what your mother always told you to do—if you can't say something good, don't say anything at all.

4. **Expect others to follow them.** This may be the hardest part. It is all too common for disappointed people to try to influence friends and family to go with them. It's one thing to lose a person or a couple. It's another thing to watch them "split the church" by actively recruiting others to go with them. Think of this likelihood as a somewhat painful blessing in disguise. Remember, those who leave would have most likely been like anchors to the reimagine process. Despite the relational pain you will experience, when oppositional people move on, it clears the path for the reimagination process to move forward with less friction. And, if you leave the door open for them to return without any shame, it is possible that once the results of the reimagination process become more tangible, they may desire to join the new, improved version of the church, perhaps even bringing with them those who followed them when they left.

These guidelines are easy to list but really, really hard to do. Because leaders are human too, and even the most seasoned of us will experience feelings of rejection, abandonment, and even betrayal when people we love choose to walk away. Here is another list of guidelines for keeping your heart healthy as you lead a process of reimagination.

1. **Maintain a healthy habit of prayer and reflecting on God's Word.** I know, it's the "Sunday School" answer that Christian leaders have to include in every list. But, seriously, neglecting our deliberate, relational habit of connecting with God leaves us vulnerable to emotional and spiritual challenges faced by every leader of a reimagination process.

2. **Remind yourself that people do not belong to you.** They belong to the Good Shepherd, and it is possible that when they leave, they are actually following His leading.

3. **Trust the ongoing stewardship of the Holy Spirit in their life.** It is exhausting when we try to usurp the work of the Holy Spirit in the lives of the people we lead. So don't do it!

4. **Deliberately connect with a group of leaders who are also leading change.** Allow this space to be a place where you confidentially vent your disappointments and frustrations. Connect with leaders in your same zip code if you can. Additionally, the Next Wave Online Community can be a connecting point for you. You can even set up your own private group with leaders you handpick to be your "foxhole friends." However, keep in mind this sage advice from Next Wave Community members Donald and Wendy Lott—"We have found that talking it over too much, over and over, just makes it bigger. Our silence can indicate that "I'm choosing trust and

moving on." Silence doesn't mean you're not in pain or hurt. We should seek out wise counsel when needed, helping us come to a place of healthy acceptance.... We have experienced fellow ministers that you can tell they never move on because fifteen years down the road, they are still venting, obviously have bitter roots, and are highly negative."

This chapter is about the reality that not everyone will stay with the church through the reimagination process. Some will leave. Some will leave negatively and loudly. Wise leaders will be emotionally and spiritually prepared for people to leave.

But not everyone who resists change will leave. Some will stay and become voices and forces of resistance to the change you are trying to lead. Most leaders will find themselves hurt by those who leave and angered by those who stay but are determined to stand in the way. What do we do about the resistors?

1. **Help them transition to another faith community.** Seriously. Kindly and directly have a conversation with them about transitioning to another faith community that is a better fit for them. To do this well, it is helpful to cultivate a strong relationship with other spiritual leaders in the community so that you can conscientiously direct people toward places where they will thrive.

2. **If possible, limit their platform for espousing their pessimism about the reimagination process.** "If possible" is the operative phrase here. Some will find their way around any efforts to limit their influence. Sometimes the best way to limit influence is to let them speak, thank them for sharing their opinion, and then move on.

3. **Relationally discover how they might become an ally instead of an opponent.** This could be the most powerful tool for managing the influence of dissenters who stay. Invite them to share a meal, actively listen to their concerns, and find ways to help them see that what they desire and where the reimagine process is headed are the same thing. You may be able to flip them from an opponent to an ally.

4. **When possible, avoid dignifying their opposition with a response.** If a response is necessary, remember, "a soft answer turns away wrath." Don't be pulled into a fight. Be meek, which means strength under control.

This chapter has been about cultivating the expectation that not everyone will be able to embrace the revitalization journey. The good news is that some people will joyfully join you in embracing a reimagined future for the church. Knowing who they are and activating them as allies will be the subject of our next chapter.

Next Wave Community Members' Reflections on Chapter Four:

Larry Grawey

> "When we began to shift our focus to pastoring our community, many people left our church. It was hard not to take them leaving personally; we had known many of them prior to starting the church. We learned early on that the church was not ours but His. I know that we all understand that on the surface, but in the midst of people leaving and finances getting tight, it can be difficult not to feel like a failure. We had to lean into prayer and, through the strength of the Spirit, stay the course, and over time, God began to bring us people who

understood the vision. He began to build new partnerships in the community and generate funds from sources that were not even on our radar. It can be difficult, but if the Holy Spirit is the one who put the vision in your heart, He will be the one to see it through."

This chapter reminded Larry of Jesus' own loss of followers recounted in John's Gospel:

When many of his disciples heard it, they said, "This is a hard saying; who can listen to it?" But Jesus, knowing in himself that his disciples were grumbling about this, said to them, "Do you take offense at this? Then what if you were to see the Son of Man ascending to where he was before? It is the Spirit who gives life; the flesh is no help at all. The words that I have spoken to you are spirit and life. But there are some of you who do not believe." (For Jesus knew from the beginning who those were who did not believe, and who it was who would betray him.) And he said, "This is why I told you that no one can come to me unless it is granted him by the Father."

After this many of his disciples turned back and no longer walked with him. So Jesus said to the twelve, "Do you want to go away as well?" Simon Peter answered him, "Lord, to whom shall we go? You have the words of eternal life, and we have believed, and have come to know, that you are the Holy One of God."

John 6:60-69 (ESV)

Not everyone who followed Jesus stayed, and He understood that. The Spirit will ask us to lead certain things that will be hard for many to understand or follow, and it is okay to let them go.

Change is hard, but you don't have to lead through it alone. Join the Next Wave Community today using the QR code below.

CHAPTER FIVE

FOCUS
Going with the Goers

The Parable of Pastor Pat

Ed showed up unannounced at Pastor Pat's office. "How come you are closing the food pantry?" Ed demanded to know. "It's been a part of the ministry of this church for decades. We can't just stop it now!" Talk about people who don't like change—Ed was Exhibit A. Despite his passion about not closing down the food pantry, Ed had never lifted a finger to help the food pantry happen. He was unaware of the fact that over the past two years, no one had been helped by the food pantry. All he knew was that he had heard it was being discontinued, and he did not like change.

Pat calmly helped Ed see the logic behind closing the pantry, and Ed begrudgingly agreed that closing the pantry was probably the right thing to do. The encounter with Ed confirmed Pat's concerns about resistance to change during the reimagination process. He was glad he had formed a plan for dealing with the naysayers in a healthy way.

Pat was ready to move on to the most positive, proactive part of the reimagination journey thus far—discovering the

members of the "Dream Team." He realized that, in many
ways, everything would rise or fall depending on the makeup
of the team. Carefully and prayerfully, he stepped into the
process of identifying his Dream Team.

How Many "Goers" Is Enough?

Erica Chenoweth was curious about the effectiveness of non-violent
protests vs. violent protests. Using the resources available to her as a
political scientist at Harvard University, she was surprised to discover
that non-violent protests achieved the outcomes desired by the protesters
51 percent of the time, while violent protests were only successful 26
percent of the time. The other surprising fact that her research uncovered
was that it took only 3.5 percent of the population directly participating
in the protests to bring about significant societal transformation.[13]

In his book *Tipping Point*, Author Malcolm Gladwell suggests the
idea of a "law of the few" playing a huge role in big societal movements.
He observes that "certain types of people are especially effective at
spreading an infectious idea, product, or behavior." In other words, it
only takes a few of the right kind of people to set a viral movement in
motion or alter the trajectory of a culture. He gives a tip of the hat to
the commonly referred 20/80 rule—20 percent of the people make 80
percent of the work happen. Anyone who has been around a church for
more than a day has seen this rule in action.

In the previous chapter, we discussed the difficult reality that not
everyone will come with you on the reimagination journey. Which begs

---

13   BBC Website, "The 3.5% Rule: How a Small Minority Can Change the World,"
      David Robson, May 13, 2019, https://www.bbc.com/future/article/20190513-
      it-only-takes-35-of-people-to-change-the-world

the question, how many allies do we need to effectively lead change? Thanks to the research of people like Erica Chenoweth and Malcolm Gladwell, we now know that the number is much smaller than we may have believed. A growing body of social research reveals the good news that setting in motion a reimagination process will not require you to gain buy-in from most of the people. In fact, the energy you exert to convince the inconvincible will likely prevent the dream of the reimagined church from becoming a reality.

All the research suggests that a dedicated and activated team of as little as 3.5 percent of your existing congregation will be enough to influence the whole group in the desired direction. This means, for example, that if your existing church is currently made up of one hundred regular participants, then you may need to discover as few as three or four solid pioneers to help you lead the reimagination process. Of course, a larger core of allies will likely accelerate the transition from the existing way of being the Church to the reimagined rhythms of the future.

You will want to cultivate a core team of allies made up of a few of the right people. Finding your "dream team" members is easy to say but challenging to do. Expectation alert—you will not get it perfect. Even Jesus invited Judas into his inner circle of disciples. No matter how hard you try and how smart you are, you will invite people to be on your team who will not live up to your expectations. However, it is possible to avoid some common selection errors. How do we find, cultivate, and activate the key team members who will embody the emerging culture of the reimagined church? That is the focus of this chapter.

Some basic guidelines for selecting your team:

1. **Don't allow them to select themselves.** For example, don't make an announcement next Sunday inviting anyone who is interested

in being part of the dream team to come to a special meeting on Sunday afternoon. This approach is almost guaranteed to end in disaster. Why? When teams are built of self-screened team members, the selection criteria are as diverse as those who have decided to join your team. Even if the special meeting is to cast vision and then invite them to join if they resonate with the vision, people tend to hear the part of the vision they want to hear and ignore the rest.

Instead, the catalyst leader (you) should take the initiative to invite potential team members to consider being part of the team. Your selection process should be informed by the guidelines shared in the remainder of this chapter.

2. **Don't be in a hurry.** The reimagination process is a marathon, not a sprint. This is really hard to do because you feel an urgency to get going. But you will never regret taking your time to get the right people on the team. Do not allow your timeline to be guided by urgency. Take the time to assess alignment and behavioral consistency (more about that in a minute). Someone has said, "Good things come to those who wait." That statement is definitely true in the team selection process.

3. **Keep your emotions in check.** Be visionary rather than reactionary. Someone may impress you with their actions or responses in a given situation, and you immediately want to get them on your team. Take the time to validate your hunches with observational evidence. Keep your options open. Be slow to invite someone to join the dream team until you've had time to fully consider their fit for the team.

4. **Recognize that the dream team predicts the future.** A frequently repeated truism used in church planting circles is crucial to the reimagining process: "The first one hundred determine the next three hundred." In other words, the earliest members of the church will have a huge amount of influence on others who choose or choose not to become part of the church. I honestly don't know if this truism has any research behind it, but it seems to align with common sense. If the first one hundred people who join a particular church are cultural cowboys, then it is reasonable to expect that as the church continues to add new members, a lot of them will be cultural cowboys.

The same is true of your dream team. The kind of people who make up your dream team will be the kind of people who become part of the reimagined church in the future. If diversity is important to you, then recruit with diversity in mind. If maturity is important to you, then recruit with maturity in mind. And so on...

Forming Your "Dream Team"

Please note—I'm using the label "dream team" as a placeholder. The actual name of the team depends totally on your specific context. Other possible labels for this group could be—allies, band of brothers, start team, catalyst group, etc. Or you may decide not to label the team at all. We are using "dream team" as a summary label to represent the leaders you intentionally invite to assist you with the process of setting in motion the reimagine journey for the church. Making the dream team a reality involves three phases—Discovering, Cultivating, and Activating. Let's consider each segment of the "dream team" formation journey.

Discovering

Jim Collins popularized the concept of getting the right people on the bus. He suggests that getting the right people on the bus precedes deciding where they will sit on the bus. Great teams are made up of solid people skillfully aligned around a common, compelling vision. It's clear—we must find the right people to lead and model the habits of the reimagined church, but how do we know who to invite in the first place?

Where to Look

It would be wonderful if all dream team members could come from the ranks of the existing church. Indeed, it is best if some of the dream team members are "natives" of the existing congregation. Natives will be able to reflect on their own personal journey of reimagination and perhaps have the relational equity needed to influence other natives toward moving in a fresh direction.

However, natives should be invited onto the dream team only if they demonstrate clear behavioral evidence that they are able to embody the heart and habits of the emerging reimagined church. Any natives who remain attached to the core heart and habits of the legacy church will significantly inhibit the forward motion of the reimagine efforts. Invite natives very carefully!

Your search criteria for the dream team should definitely include some immigrants—people from outside the legacy church that you have invited because you know their behavior embodies the heart and habits of the reimagined church. While immigrants do have a disadvantage due to their lack of relational connections with the existing members, the right immigrants bring huge advantages to the dream team and reimagination efforts.

Those advantages include the following: 1) they are more loyal to the future than they are to the past; 2) they typically have a stronger relational connection to you; 3) they are unencumbered by sentimental feelings toward unhelpful missional behaviors from the past.

Who to Look For

First—Look for people of character. Character is "king." The temptation to make talent king is common, but we will always regret that decision. Character is known in two ways—direct observation or referral. In other words, to make a meaningful character judgment, you must personally spend time with the person or know someone trustworthy who can serve as a character witness. Discerning character is more of an art than a science. By nature, it is very subjective and intuitive. Prayer must be part of the discernment process. Once you've prayed, observed, received referrals, and prayed some more, if you have the slightest doubt, it is better to be safe than sorry.

If you are married, you have access to a valuable added perspective in the process of character discernment. Your spouse. Wise leaders listen to the insights of their spouses. At one point in my ministry, I had a team member who I thought was outstanding. He was very gifted and always seemed to say the right things publicly and privately. I had no reason to see him as a liability in any way. One night, I woke up to find my wife quietly sobbing. I asked her what was wrong. She said, "I don't trust (name of the leader). I think he's going to hurt you." I asked her why she felt that way, and she could only point to a hunch. I was shocked and unsettled. I immediately began to pay much closer attention to what was going on with this particular leader and soon discovered some very serious character flaws that had been hidden under the surface. Ultimately, it led to a very painful process that resulted in his removal from leadership. Take discernment of character seriously.

Second—Chemistry matters. A lot. By chemistry, I mean how the person interacts with others and especially how they function in a team environment. Like character, this is a trait best observed in real life and in real time. You may find some assistance with observing chemistry through the use of tools like an Emotional Intelligence Assessment. But, like character, good old-fashioned direct observation will go a long way toward helping you get a sense of how they will contribute to the positive health of a team (or not).

Third—Compatibility. Compatibility has to do with how they get along with the vision. Are they compatible with the direction the reimagine process is taking the church? Do they find it hard to let go of old habits and adapt to new ones? Compatibility is about alignment with the emerging heart and habits of the reimagined church.

Fourth—Calling. Calling is the undeniable "set apartness" that gives a leader an awareness of God's direction in their life. Calling is perhaps the most difficult characteristic to accurately discern, but it will show up as tenacity toward the mission, passion for the cause, and a willingness to go above and beyond. Called people project a sense of being on a mission from God and are difficult to discourage. They know that they know that they know that what they are doing is what God wants them to be doing.

Fifth—Consistency—By consistency, we mean emotional and mental stability. Consistent people have a track record of handling the ups and downs of life in healthy ways. They are intentional about surrounding themselves with good friends and colleagues with whom they can process the difficulties that life throws their way. They rejoice with those who rejoice and mourn with those who mourn.

Sixth—Competency—Competency means they can do what needs to be done. The dream team must be proficient at making disciples. Competency is focusing on what people actually do. It does not care about their philosophical positions. It only cares about what they actually do. Assessing competency is based on the sociological principle that "past performance predicts future behavior." In other words, how a person has tended to act in the past is how they will tend to act in the future. Like the other characteristics, competency is best observed directly, but it is also possible to assess competency indirectly by asking the potential team member to share how they have exhibited competency in the past. For example, if you want to know if someone is an effective evangelist, you can ask them to tell you about the last person they led to Christ.

Conducting a behaviorally focused interview is the best way to assess competence. Think of the competencies that will be needed for a person to add value to the dream team. Some of those might include being a habitual disciple maker, maintaining healthy relationships, exhibiting tenacity, being a great team player, etc. Think about the actual behaviors that indicate the competencies are present. For example—behavioral evidence that a person is highly competent in maintaining healthy relationships would be the person has a group of close friends who connect often to share life, has friends across a spectrum from very close to soft acquaintances, is regularly meeting new people, is a reliable friend, etc. To discover their level of competency, ask them to share actual stories of how they have made and kept friends.

The Ideal Dream Team member profile: Keeping the six characteristic categories in mind, prepare the profile of the ideal team member. The ideal profile should be a very high bar that few, if any, can live up to. This profile is for your use only and should never be shared with others. It is a tool to help you decide who to invite onto the dream team. If you feel uncomfortable pursuing such a high standard, remember that the initial team sets the mold for all the additional community members to come. The beginning of the process is when you have the most opportunity to shape the foundational team culture.

Cultivating Your Dream Team

After you have created the initial list of potential dream team members, it's time to cultivate your dream team. You will be tempted to share the whole vision for the reimagined church and ask them to commit to it right out of the gate. However, your initial interactions with them should be one-on-one and informal. Your purpose in meeting with them will be to confirm the assessment you have made of them, not to ask them to be on the team. Are they indeed the people you want to build the culture of the reimagined church with? What are the natural behaviors of their life? How are they currently using their time? Does what you see and hear confirm or conflict with your initial assessment?

The cultivation process will likely look like a lot of shared meals and activities that give space for conversation and listening. After you've spent time with individuals and couples listening to, observing, and hearing stories from their lives, the final list of your initial dream team will begin to come into focus for you. Pray over the list one more time and ask God to help you know what you can't know. Listen carefully to the voice of the Spirit and then make your list of dream team invitees.

Activating the Prototype

Once you feel confident with the potential roster, it's time to begin the process of onboarding them to the vision of the reimagined church.

Guidelines for inviting people to join the dream team:

1. **Invite personally.** Don't invite people to the dream team using any form of public announcement, email blast, social media post, etc. It is important that you choose the people who will join you on this journey. Invitation is best done one on one and face to face. Share with them why you think they are qualified to be part of the dream team.

2. **Under-promise.** You know the classic phrase "under promise and over deliver." That's excellent advice when forming a dream team. Avoid grand sweeping statements that conjure up visions of unrealistic outcomes. Keep your invite simple and grounded.

3. **Manage expectations.** As concisely as possible, explain to them what you will be expecting of them as members of the dream team. For example, "We will meet every Tuesday night at my house for two hours." Be as specific as possible. However, help them know that since this is a "learn as we go" situation, the schedule may need to be adjusted and they will be invited to give input to future midcourse corrections.

4. **Preferred future.** Clearly describe a compelling picture of the preferred future. Revisit Chapter Two: "The End," reflect on the picture of the future you form there, and put together a simple paragraph that summarizes the key elements of the vision of the reimagined church. Note! Do not contrast it with the existing form of the church. Instead, describe a possible community rhythm that you are inviting the dream team to join you in building. It can be helpful to list the elements of the future church in bullet point format.

For example:
- Imagine a faith community of disciples actively helping everyone around them move toward Jesus and become more like Jesus.
- Imagine forming an ecosystem of redemptive practices that result in a flourishing economy and a rising level of emotional health in the greater community.
- Imagine a spiritual environment centered on the way of Jesus so clearly that everyone in proximity responds with curiosity, interest, and wonder.
- Imagine being part of a cohort of disciple-makers who empower everyone around them to bless the world with the best version of themselves.

The statements above are sample "template" statements to help spark your imagination about how to paint a preferred picture of the future that is compelling. The picture you create for your dream team should specifically reference actual potential impacts on your specific community. For example, "a 50 percent reduction in the number of single moms with no relational and practical support." Or "a 25 percent reduction in the crime rate." Or "every parentless child in our zip code has access to a foster family." Statements like these will help everyone see how the future can be shaped.

5. **Experiment!** Constantly use the word "experiment." Be sure to frequently include it in your conversation with potential dream team members. They need to know that you will be making simple and possibly significant adjustments along the way. Compelling pictures of the future are rarely accurate in every detail. Be sure they understand that the dream team will be learning together as they go.

6. **Exit lanes.** Create convenient and frequent exits. Ask for a specific time commitment that is long enough for them to really learn and unlearn the necessary habits to support the future church but short enough that they can step off the dream team graciously if they turn out to no longer feel called. This approach provides a time of stability as you begin the reimagination process, but it also provides a structured way for people to discontinue their involvement in a minimally disruptive manner.

7. **New habits.** Begin practicing the new habits of the reimagined church. Once you've established the initial dream team, it's time to bring them together. The meetings and activities of the dream team should not be shared in any public forum. The dream team is not secret, but as much as possible, you want to keep it off the radar screen of the existing church members who have not been invited to be on the dream team. Dream team members should ideally meet at times and places that are outside the scope of the existing church calendar. With that in mind, the dream team

should not be a Sunday School class, a small group listed on the small group roster, a midweek meeting program, etc.

Get Real

This dream team that you have pulled together will become the collective architects of the reimagined church. They will be working together with you to breathe life into the picture of the future you seek to make a reality. This group must be characterized by action, not just philosophical discussions and conversations. Each dream team member must see themselves as the embodiment of the preferred vision of the future for the church. Chapter Seven will provide some specific structure and guidelines for activating your dream team members. But first, let's think together about what to do with the church members who are NOT part of the dream team.

> *Join the Next Wave Community today using the QR code below to learn how other church leaders recruited their dream teams.*

CHAPTER SIX

STABILIZE
Continue Church as Usual

The Parable of Pastor Pat

As they drove home from the restaurant, Pat looked at his wife and smiled. "The Bensons are going to be a great addition to the team," he commented. She returned his smile and agreed. "They really are special. Until we went through this process, I had no idea how much gold God has blessed us with."

Over the last two months, Pastor Pat had enjoyed the process of developing his "Dream Team." He'd successfully identified a group that was about 10 percent of the number of people in the congregation. He believed that a third of that group was absolutely all in. Thinking about the future was fun again.

But Pat knew that for the future to actually be fun, he would need to help the existing church continue to move forward. All of his studies and past experiences had led him to believe that making the transition from the present church to the future church was going to test the full spectrum of his leadership skills. He knew that for a season, he would need to wear two very different hats simultaneously. He was headed into territory where he'd never been before.

Back in the 90s, I attended an event at Mile High Stadium in Denver. It was an incredible experience. It was also my first and last time in the venerable stadium. The stadium was well-known partially due to its designation of being situated at an altitude of 5280 feet—one mile high. As I made my way to my seat, it was easy to see that the years had not been kind to this aging icon. Built in 1948, it appeared to be nearing the end of its usefulness as a venue for big events.

Sure enough, a few years later, plans were announced to build a new stadium for the Denver Broncos. I wondered where the new stadium would be located. The options inside the city were limited. The developers of the new stadium encountered a lot of resistance to moving the stadium outside of the actual Denver city limits. After all, they are the DENVER Broncos. After much careful study and deliberation, the decision was made—to build the new stadium in the parking lot of the old stadium!

And so, for one season, the Broncos continued to play in the original Mile High Stadium while their new home was being built just fifty feet away from their existing home. In fact, for a short time, Denver was home to two full-size football stadiums right next to each other.

In this chapter, we will be suggesting a strategic approach to reimagining the church that has some parallels to the solution that the Denver Broncos utilized to replace the Mile High stadium. The Broncos didn't tear down the old stadium until the new stadium was ready for use. By doing so, they solved several challenges before they became serious problems.

Challenge #1 – If the existing stadium was torn down, where would the Broncos play their home games?

Challenge #2 – If the Broncos couldn't play home games, how would they remain competitive and profitable as an NFL team?

Challenge #3 – Part of the allure of Mile High Stadium is that it is literally built on land that has an elevation of exactly 5280 feet. If they rebuild the stadium in another location, will the new location have the same panache as the old location?

Challenge #4 – If the Broncos couldn't play in their stadium, what would happen to their consecutive "sold out" streak of selling every seat in the stadium for every game since 1970?

I do realize this may be a little bit of a stretch, but humor me as I suggest that the challenges of a reimagination process in a local church are similar to the challenges faced by the Broncos in their quest to replace their aging stadium.

Church Challenge #1 – What happens to the existing congregation when the reimagined church becomes a reality?

Church Challenge #2 – If the existing church suddenly ceases its expected rhythms, how will the ministry be funded?

Church Challenge #3 – The culture of the existing church is strong and valued by the members. How will the new reimagined church be skillfully formed without disrespecting the past?

Church Challenge #4 – If the existing church no longer meets in its accustomed manner, will the surrounding community perceive it as a failure?

All of these "existing church" challenges are created by the tension of leading a church in a new direction. Embedded in existing church culture is the idea that significant changes must be introduced to all members of the existing congregation at the same time. Everyone must buy into the new vision for the church. Everyone must participate in it. This idea is based on anecdotes of outlier churches that managed to find a way to reimagine themselves as a collective and leads to some renewal practices that are almost always destined to fail because it violates a well-established sociological principle—the theory of diffusion of innovation.

Diffusion of innovation was popularized by sociologist Everett Rogers as a way to explain the rate at which new ideas and technology spread. Rogers identified five adopter categories that help leaders understand what to expect while leading an organization through change.

The "adoption of innovation" categories are as follows:

Innovators – They are primed to be the first to embrace innovation. Innovators will typically be about 2.5 percent of the total number of people in an organization.

Early Adopters – They tend to be comfortable with change and adopting new ideas. Rogers says this group will be made up of about 13.5 percent of the total number of people in an organization.

Early Majority – They adopt new innovations before the average person. However, evidence that the new innovation works is needed before people in this category will embrace the innovation. This group is commonly composed of 34 percent of the total number of people in the organization.

Late Majority – They are skeptical of change and will only adopt new innovations when they are generally accepted by the majority of the people in the organization. These folks make up about 34 percent of the total number of people in an organization.

Laggards – They are very conservative and strongly prefer that things stay the same as they have always been. They are always the last to change and are the hardest group to appeal to. Laggards typically make up about 16 percent of the total number of people in a group.

You've probably already grasped the challenge that this sociological principle creates. The pivotal category in every organization is the 34 percent of the people who make up the "Early Majority." But they must see evidence that the new innovation will work before they will jump on the bandwagon of change. Without the blessing of the "Early Majority," people from the "Late Majority" and "Laggard" categories will never adopt the innovation and the reimagine process will fail.

The key to leading a successful reimagination process is creating "evidence that the new innovation works." Creating that evidence is the role of the "Innovators" and "Early Adopters." These are the people you want on your dream team. They will create the habits of the reimagined church so that others can see the desired future and be motivated to move from the comfort zone of what they know into the blessing of being part of the reimagined church. We will discuss how to skillfully activate "Innovators" and "Early Adopters" in the chapters to come.

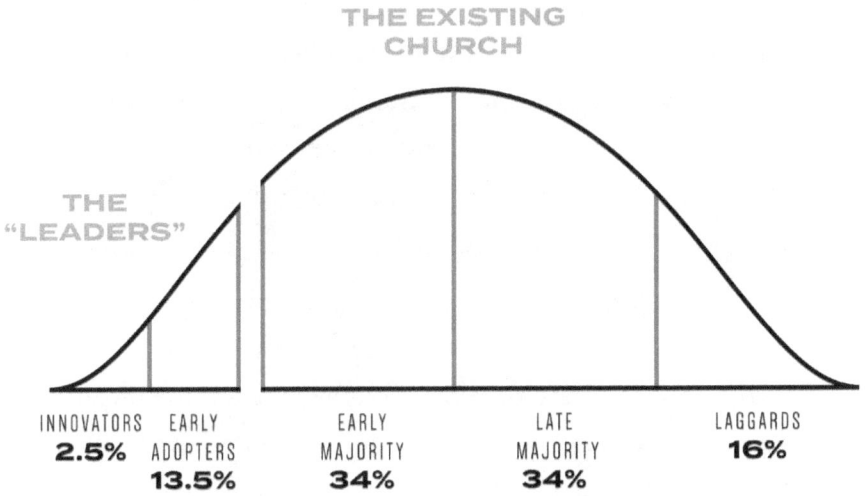

But this chapter is about keeping the Early/ Late Adopters plus the Laggards engaged while the Innovators and Early Adopters are creating the future. You've got to keep the old stadium working while the new stadium is being built. Otherwise, the Early/Late Adopters and Laggards will perceive the new as a threat to the habits of church that they love just the way it is and they will resist the new. Although the resistance will typically be passive in nature, it will be formidable because the Early/Late Adopters and Laggards make up 84 percent of the people of the organization. If 84 percent of the people do not participate in the behavioral changes needed for the reimagined church to become a reality, you will not be successful in reimagining the church.

How to Stabilize the Existing Church While Innovating

Don't change anything unless you absolutely have to.

As much as possible, keep all of the existing meetings and rhythms of the existing church intact. Don't alter the worship service schedule or style. If you have other weekly meetings (such as a mid-week Bible study or Sunday evening worship service), keep them going without any visible changes. If changes are absolutely necessary, make them slowly over time.

A well-known church legend illustrates how to make incremental changes. A legacy church had a beautiful old organ that no one knew how to play and was incompatible with the music genre of the church. Every time the church gathered, the organ sat in a prominent place on the platform, reminding the attendees of the past and taking up a lot of space on the platform that could be used for other purposes. The pastor and most of the church leaders decided the organ needed to be moved from the platform. The leadership team knew that many of the church members held strong sentimental feelings toward the organ. Moving it abruptly was not the better part of wisdom. The pastor decided to move the organ one foot at a time. Over several months, the organ slowly migrated to a less prominent place on the platform. Eventually, it was in the corner of the platform. The next week, it was draped with a cloth that was the same color as the wall behind it. The next week, the organ was gone. No one noticed.

Reduce the energy you are giving to existing church habits.

In order to keep the rhythm and habits of the existing church, as well as your sanity, intact, you will need to strategically reduce the amount of energy you are personally giving to leading the existing church. It is unwise to attempt to power through and continue to be the prime leader responsible for all the demands of both the existing church and the emerging reimagined church. Almost every leader thinks they can succeed at giving maximum energy to both the existing and emerging church. Few succeed.

The best way to reduce the amount of energy you are giving to the existing church is to delegate that responsibility to others. The transition from your hands-on leadership to fully delegated leadership should be incremental to reduce any sense of shock to the loyal members of the existing congregation. The transition time frame depends on how dependent the existing members are on your direct involvement and attention in the normal rhythms and habits of the church. If delegation and leadership development have been an ongoing part of your leadership approach, then the transition time can be relatively brief. However, if your congregation is accustomed to you doing everything, the transition time will likely be longer.

Here is a non-exhaustive list of the rhythms and habits that might be delegated to others and continued throughout the duration of the reimagine process:

- Hospital visitation,
- Weekly worship leading
- Weekly Sunday sermon prep and preaching
- Weekly Bible studies and small groups
- Counseling ministries, weddings, funerals, etc.

However long the transition timeframe is, the desired outcome is that you will be freed up to direct most of your energy to living out, modeling, and leading the habits of the reimagined church.

Keep space between the emerging new and existing church practices.

Many leaders of reimagination processes are so eager to see the new rhythms and habits emerge that they begin to prematurely merge the practices of the new and the old together. This may feel like the right thing to do, but in most cases, this will only confuse everyone. Notice that we have inserted a gap between the "Innovators/Early Adopters" in the Innovation Curve Diagram. During the formation phases of the reimagined church, these two groups need to be strategically segregated from each other. The existing church members need to feel at home in the church they have known. The members of the dream team need to be able to fully live out the practices of the emerging church without having to explain themselves to the members of the existing church.

THE REIMAGINE PROCESS

The purpose of this transitional segregation is to allow both groups space to worship in a manner that resonates with them. How you lead this can be fairly simple. For example, Dream Team meetings or events should be scheduled at times that do not conflict with the normally scheduled meeting times of the church. If the existing church has some form of Sunday School classes or small groups, Dream Team meetings can be scheduled as one of the options during that time frame. Dream Team members should be encouraged to attend the normal weekly gathering of the existing church to minimize any disruption that the members of the existing church may feel. But, like you, Dream Team members should also be encouraged to decrease the amount of time and energy they are giving to support the regular activities of the existing church.

> *Do note that you don't want to discount the power of preaching to the existing church with the new model in mind. The existing church may not be there yet, but the vision of a preferred future can be woven into your messaging. You are potentially preparing the ground for the merger of the old and the new.*
>
> *–Larry Grawey.*

Deliberately increase personal connections with existing church members in a low-energy way.

I realize this suggestion sounds like a contradiction of all the previous points. Let's unpack this one a little bit. Many leaders underestimate the value that faithful church attendees place on their connectivity to the key congregational leader. Shifting energy to give maximum time and attention to the Dream Team will inevitably mean that your face-to-face availability for existing church members will decrease. They will notice. So what to do? Early on in the process, begin to replace your face-to-face habits with connection points that can be done remotely. For example, a monthly customized personal email sent to each existing church member. By customized, I mean embedding in the email something unique to the person receiving the note. Something like, "I want you to know that I'm praying for your mom as she undergoes surgery next week." The task of actually compiling and sending out the emails can be delegated to a trusted assistant. The key point of this concept is to creatively find ways to replace direct face time with personalized connections that help people feel seen and cared for.

The result of all this is that during the reimagine transition time, if all goes well, you will end up leading two distinct churches operating simultaneously alongside each other. One church will be the relatively undisturbed existing church. The other church will be the thoughtfully emerging reimagined church. Leadership of the existing church should be transitioned to trusted delegated leaders. Your main energy should be directed toward leading the emerging reimagined church.

The existence of the emerging church should not necessarily be a secret kept from the members of the existing church. However, the activities and actions of the reimagined church should not be communicated to the members of the existing church via general announcement methods such as newsletters, group emails, public website, or verbal announcements at regular gatherings. Since the Dream Team will likely be only a small number of individuals (perhaps 16 percent compared to 84 percent), the Dream Team can legitimately be referred to as some sort of specialized small group. When any of the existing church members ask about the actions and activities of the reimagined church, your response can simply be that it is an invitation-only small group. However, since most of the activities of the Dream Team will happen outside the typical schedule of the existing church, the activities and meetings of the Dream Team will naturally tend to stay off the radar of the members of the existing church.

How long will the church be in this transitional phase? As long as is necessary for the creation of compelling "evidence that the new innovation works." Depending on the specific context, the transitional time frame could be a few months but could also be as long as a couple of years.

Indicators That You May Be Nearing the End of the Transitional Phase

- Your dream team members have established new and desirable patterns of living out their faith in Jesus.
- Your dream team members have no desire to go back to the previous patterns and habits of living out their faith.
- The existing congregation members have become positively aware of the reimagined life patterns of your Dream Team members.
- Your existing congregation members are asking a lot of curious questions about what's going on with your specialized small group.

As you prepare yourself and your church for the reimagination process, you will need to keep the old stadium operational while the new stadium is being built. Please don't tear down the old stadium before you're ready to play in the new one. This will only lead to heartache and frustration for everyone. Ironically, the best way forward is to strategically split the church and skillfully lead both sides of the split!

This chapter has been focused on how to stabilize the existing church through the transition phase of the reimagining process. Before we discuss how to introduce the new innovations to the members of the existing congregation, we need to shine our spotlight on how to maximize the journey of the dream team during the transition phase of the reimagine process. That will be the subject of our next chapter.

Interested in hearing some success (and not-so-success) stories about the transition phase? Join the Next Wave Community today using the QR code below.

PART THREE

GO

Congratulations—you're ready. Now it's time to GO! We are moving from the preparation phase into the execution phase of the reimagination process. If the reimagination process was a building, we would be moving from laying the foundation to beginning to put up the walls. Over the next four chapters, we will describe how to make the reimagination process a reality.

CHAPTER SEVEN

EXPERIMENT
Joyfully Failing Forward

The Parable of Pastor Pat

Pat had dreaded this particular board meeting more than any before. He knew if it didn't go well, all the reimagine dreams would be dashed. To increase the probability of a good outcome, Pat had spent the weeks leading up to the meeting personally visiting with each individual member of the board. He wanted them to be aware of his plans and give the green light for the basic concept of the reimagination journey.

He kept his description of the future deliberately ambiguous but shared the real outcomes he hoped to achieve. More disciples made. More veteran believers activated as disciple-makers. A stronger connection with the greater community. A growing number of people far from God deciding to follow Jesus. He painted the picture and then asked for the board to affirm the general direction. His efforts to prepare the board members for the meeting paid off. They were ready to say yes to the basic steps that Pat proposed to implement the process of reimagination.

Now it was time to activate the goers while at the same time providing solid ministry care to the faithful members of the existing church. It was about to get interesting.

"I've missed more than 9,000 shots in my career. I've lost almost 300 games. Twenty-six times, I've been trusted to the game-winning shot and missed. I've failed over and over and over again in my life. And that is why I succeed."

–Michael Jordan

The existing church is humming along mostly undisturbed. Your picture of the future reimagined church is as sharp and clear as it can be at this point. It's time to identify and activate your Dream Team and begin to take your first steps toward making the reimagined church a reality. This is where it gets really fun—and really dangerous. Fun because you have created an environment where you are free to try new ministry approaches unfettered by pushback from the naysayers. Dangerous because not all of the concepts and ideas you dream about will result in the reimagined church you are envisioning. This is the "Go" phase of the reimagination process. Speculative theories must leap off the whiteboard and be fleshed out in real everyday life. This is where the imagined begins to become tangible.

How do you, as the title of this chapter describes, begin to try stuff joyfully failing forward? Here are some guiding principles for translating the dream into the real everyday walking-around life of the church.

1. **Call everything an experiment. We've suggested this in an earlier chapter, but it's worth repeating. Everything should be allowed to fail.** There's nothing new about this concept. You've heard it before. Maybe even done it. Perhaps you've even done it well. But just in case you feel a tinge of skepticism when you hear

that advice, here are some thoughts about how to experiment effectively.

a. The heart of this concept is managing expectations skillfully. What people expect actually influences how they perceive their experience. Two people going to the same event can come away with completely different reactions to the event based on their expectations going in. Be careful to manage the expectations of your dream team well.

b. Carefully craft how you talk about the future church in a way that sets the early adopters up to perceive the emerging church in a positive light. The word "experiment" is helpful because it leaves room for uncertainty about the outcome while at the same time excitement about where the church is going.

c. "Experiments" can be successful, but, ironically, they can also be viewed as a success when the experiment fails. "We are learning together" is a phrase to keep on the tip of your tongue as you lead a group through any missional experiment. Learning together goes hand in hand with making everything an experiment and gives you space to fail and try other experiments.

2. **Be relentless in keeping this new foundation oriented around the vision of Jesus for His Church.** One of the dangers of a reimagination process is that the guiding vision of the future can be inspired by superficial factors that have nothing to do with joining Jesus on His Mission. Our own model preferences are the most common distractions that pull well-intentioned

churches off their mission. The question is not what new models of being the church do we prefer? But how are disciples best made in this ministry context? Start with the second question. If the answer to the second question also happens to be the answer to the first question, then you will be blessed with less resistance on the reimagine journey. But if the answer is different, then you will need to jettison your preferred model and adopt the modality that results in disciples being made because that is what the church exists to do.

3. **Take your time.** A fresh vision for the future is invigorating. It makes you want to get there NOW! The temptation is to force the new reality into existence by taking shortcuts. Here's another piece of wisdom that gets tossed around and abused a lot. "It's a marathon, not a sprint." The parallel truth is, "If you run a marathon like a sprint, you will lose." Pushing too hard too fast is the undoing of many well-crafted reimagination plans. Give adequate time for the "dream team" to make the habits of the reimagined church part of their personal DNA. It won't be weeks. Probably not months. Might be a year. Could even be longer.

4. **Facilitate a learning community culture.** Facilitation skills are becoming more common in the leadership development paths of ministry leaders. But many veteran leaders have only been schooled in the art of proclamation. They know how to put a good, well-rounded message together, but they struggle to lead a group of people through a discovery process. To truly be "experimental," the emerging model must be the product of people learning together. Here are some key guidelines for facilitating a learning community.

a. Early on, take time to help everyone arrive at clarity regarding the "why" of the group. Why are we here? Seek agreement around this question first. Then, go to the deeper question of "what is it about the purpose of this group that makes me want to be part of it?" Honestly processing the "why" of the group coupled with the "why" of the participant may result in some of the team members realizing they should not be part of the group. Don't view this as a bad thing. It's a blessing because the remaining group will be more unified around the "why?" Knowing their personal "why" will help keep them motivated when the going gets tough.

b. Renew your commitment to good coaching skills. By now, most leaders in the American church have been exposed to the basic concepts of coaching. The practice of good coaching skills is the foundation of well-executed facilitation. As a coach/facilitator, your function is to help the group discover how to move from where they are to the agreed-upon destination of the reimagined church.

c. Avoid getting trapped in a non-stop cycle of facilitation. When it is clear that a consensus has emerged, take off your facilitator hat, put on your healthy leader hat, and declare where the reimagination process is going.

5. **Activate leaders around the habits and practices of the emerging church.**

Your vision of the future will include the emergence of a community of activated disciple-makers, all empowered to disciple the next generation of activated disciple-makers.

Moving toward a culture of disciple-making will necessitate a lot of learning and unlearning of habits. Old habits of viewing disciple-making as a class to be taken will die hard. New habits of seeing every interaction with anyone as potentially a micro expression of the disciple-making journey will feel unnatural at first, like signing your name with your non-dominant hand. The dream team needs to be constantly reminded that they are the pioneers of the reimagined church.

At first, the habits of the reimagined church will feel awkward and even unnatural. Perhaps even wrong. I remember the first time I found myself in a spiritual conversation with a self-proclaimed atheist on a Sunday morning. My old habit would have been to offer that person the opportunity to listen to my sermon! This new habit felt wrong. But over time, my encounters with people who felt far from God now feel normal, whenever and wherever they occur. Your dream team members may go through similar withdrawal symptoms as they begin to live a life built on a platform of disciple-making.

6.   **Be deliberate about naming and unlearning unhelpful habits.**
     "Spiritual progress is not attained by a formula of knowing plus knowing plus knowing. Despite what we may assume, spiritual growth is not the result of endless addition. Spiritual growth also requires subtraction. Spiritual progress is not knowing, knowing, knowing; spiritual progress is more often knowing, unknowing, new knowing."
     –Brian Zahnd, "When Everything's on Fire."[14]

14   Brian Zahnd, *When Everything's on Fire*, (Downers Grove, IL: Intervarsity Press, November 2021), 76.

I'm doubling down on this point because it is where so many reimagination efforts fail to take hold. Breaking unhelpful habits does not happen accidentally. This is one of the great benefits of keeping the dream team segregated from the ongoing rhythm of the existing congregation. If the dream team members attempt to discover and put into practice the rhythms of the reimagined church while at the same time continuing full engagement with the rhythms of the existing church, they will find themselves tangled up in the expectations and constraints associated with the habits of the existing church. The dream team needs space to "unknow" so they can experience "new knowing." The cloistered setting of the dream team becomes a safe place to name the habits of the existing church that are standing in the way of the reimagined church.

For example, you and the dream team members have determined that holding typical Sunday morning worship gatherings will not be a part of the rhythm of the emerging reimagined church because the Sunday morning time frame has significant built-in scheduling conflicts with the people in the community you are trying to reach. That reality needs to be named and unlearned. You acknowledge that Sunday morning is not an optimal time for connecting with lost people and recognize that Thursday night at 8 p.m. is an optimal time.

7. **Incorporate appropriate habits from the existing church.** It is also important to acknowledge that the existing church may have many attributes that need to be carried forward and incorporated into the reimagined church. Not every practice of the existing church is unhelpful. Doing a thorough audit of the practices of the existing church will help you and the dream team

recognize the habits that should be carried forward or unlearned. Be very intentional about the habits you choose to carry on. They must fit inside the agreed-upon "why" of the emerging reimagined church. Every habit of the reimagined church must be intentional, not just a favorite habit carried forward from the existing church.

8. **Pass along the new rhythms to at least the third generation.** Generation 1 – You do it. Generation 2 – You help someone else do it. Generation 3 –You help someone help someone else do it. This is how practices become viral. Doing "it" is great, but if it stops with you alone, it will fall short of the hoped-for Kingdom potential. "It" is making disciples—and whatever model of the church you are imagining—to be a biblically faithful church, it must be built on the foundation of activated disciples who make activated disciples who make activated disciples. Seeing it through to the third generation is important because when the practice of disciple-making reaches the third generation, it is highly probable that disciple-making is embedded into the DNA of the reimagined church and will continue to be reproduced in the succeeding generations.

I saw this dramatically demonstrated during a weeklong visit with Ralph Moore and the leadership team of Hope Chapel. During a visit with the members of a Hope Chapel "mini-church," it dawned on me that everyone in the circle had been a believer for less than a year—including the leader. It was also clear that their understanding of what it meant to follow Jesus was that they would be actively involved in making disciples every day. They had never been church "spectators," content to watch the show passively from the pews. They truly believed that it was normal for every believer to be intentionally involved in making disciples of the people around them every day as they lived their lives. *They didn't know any better.* When they brought someone to Jesus, they helped them bring others to Jesus because in their minds, that's what Christians do.

With the guidelines above as your guardrails, it's time to pull your dream team together and begin to practice being the reimagined church. The sequence of the emergence of the reimagined church may look something like this:

1. **You do it first.** As much as possible, incorporate the known practices and rhythms of the reimagined church into your own life. This means you will need to skillfully delegate detailed responsibility for leading the existing church to other leaders. (More about that in the next chapter.)

2. **Recruit followers.** You invite others to join you in practicing the new habits of the reimagined church. Once the habits of the reimagined church become normal to you, invite others to join you in living out the new habits. Some or all of your Dream Team may need to delegate their leadership responsibilities for the existing church to others.

3. **Live out the reimagined rhythms.** As a collective, the dream team members live out the new practices until they become the normal way of being the church for the members of the dream team.

4. **Prepare to invite others into the reimagined life.** This is when the practices of the reimagined church may safely be made known to the members of the existing church.

The sequence above describes the phase of the reimagination process when you will virtually have two churches operating alongside each other simultaneously (as we illustrated in the previous chapter). Here is a sample of what the schedule of a church in the "Parallel Church" phase might look like.

> **Sunday morning** – Existing Church meets as usual, led mostly by delegated leaders working cooperatively with the leadership team. Reimagined church members are encouraged to attend this gathering.
>
> **Sunday evening** – Reimagined Church meets for training, worship, and vision casting.
>
> **Monday** – Existing Church has no regularly scheduled events. Reimagined Church leaders are encouraged to use Monday night as a potential time to spontaneously connect with people who feel far from God.
>
> **Tuesday** – No events scheduled for either church. However, reimagined church leaders are encouraged to devote extra time on Tuesday to praying by name for the people in their sphere of influence.
>
> **Wednesday** – Existing Church has the normal Wednesday night Bible study. Reimagined Church meets as a small group to practice **Christian ordinances** and celebrate missional progress

Thursday –No events scheduled for either church. Reimagined Church members are encouraged to find a non-church social context in which to cultivate redemptive relationships.

Friday – No all-church events scheduled regularly for either church. However, Reimagined church leaders are encouraged to be alert for recreational activities they can participate in that place them life on life with people who are not yet following Jesus.

Saturday – Once per month, a connection time may be scheduled on Saturdays that brings together the existing church members along with the members of the reimagined church.

As you can see, the transition phase will require a high degree of commitment from the members of the reimagined church. This reality is important to share with them as you recruit them to be part of the dream team. Keep in mind that this is a sample intended to help you begin to translate what you are dreaming about into actionable practices and habits. What you decide to do in your context may be completely different from the pattern above.

Trying Stuff and Failing Well

The title of this chapter is "Joyfully Failing Forward." What are some experiments you might try? Remember to start with the question, *"How do we best make disciples in this context?"* With that question as your guiding value, look around at the emerging options popping up all around you. If you've postured your dream team well, you've created some margin to experiment with the many emerging forms of the Church. Have you been curious about the "Dinner Church" movement? Now is the time to give it a shot. Wondering about launching a digital expression of the church? This is your chance to see if this approach will increase the missional capacity of the church. Inspired by the Tampa or Kansas City Underground models of church? Design and deploy experiments that help you see the relevance of these church models. Intrigued by the Brave Cities approach of Hugh Halter and Taylor McCall? Learn everything you can from them and see if it resonates with your situation. Has God placed a dream in your heart for a church rhythm no one has ever seen before? You've set yourself and your dream team up to turn a dream into a reality.

Here's the true beauty of this approach—while you are experimenting with "new stuff" off to the side, the existing church can continue along doing and being the church in a familiar, stable, and predictable way. Instead of issuing an ultimatum that causes people to accept or reject a new-fangled form of church that scares them, the reimagined church process we are describing sets an existing church up to experience the best of both worlds.

Some Thoughts about "Failing Forward"

The American Church has a very specific challenge when it comes to failing forward. A strong American cultural value is winning. And winning some more. The idea that failure is not an option is drilled into us from our earliest years. On our way to being winners, the idea that failing equals losing got tangled up in our psyche. As a result, we tend to only try stuff when success is guaranteed. This cultural value works against us when we set out to reimagine our church.

It is essential to keep in mind that when you try new approaches, not everything you do will work. You may even fail spectacularly! Elon Musk is a twenty-first-century uber entrepreneur who has successfully started a number of game-changing corporations. Whether he's building Tesla vehicles, assembling rockets bound for Mars, or launching satellites to provide high-speed internet to the most remote places on Earth, Elon Musk builds failure into his expectations. Space X rockets have exploded numerous times. But the lessons learned from the exploding rockets have propelled Space X into being the most prolific player in the space industry. Period. No country or any other space company even comes close. Winston Churchill said, "Success is not final, failure is not fatal: it is the courage to continue that counts." My guess is that Elon Musk would agree.

In order to successfully reimagine the church you lead, you will likely have to blow up some rockets. Failure goes hand in hand with trying new approaches.

Here are some guiding ideas that will help you fail well as you experiment with fresh ways of being with Jesus on His Mission.

1. **Manage expectations.** Expectations go a long way in determining our perception of reality. Carefully calibrate the expectations of your dream team by intentionally under-promising and doing your best to over-deliver. If your dream team expects to set in motion a multiplication movement that changes the world within the next five years, they will be disappointed. But if they expect to try to find ways to make disciples and expect that the ways they try will work sometimes and fail other times, then their expectations will likely be calibrated just about right.

2. **Calculate the worst-case scenario.** It's okay to ask the question, "What's the worst that could happen?" If you are able to live the worst, then the risk is worth it. If the worst is more than you can handle, then put the experiment on the shelf.

3. **Seek to learn from every failure.** When a failure does happen, lead the way in learning everything you can about why it happened and then be deliberate about incorporating the learning into the next experiment.

4. **Build the possibility of failure into your definition of success.** "The history of rocket development is one which is replete with failure and where there are very few successes. We hope to be one of those successes, but something that I want to make sure everyone's aware of is that no matter what happens on launch day, I feel that we have really been quite successful already." –Elon Musk. See what he did there? Communicate with your dream team in a manner that helps them view failure as a necessary part of the pathway to success.

5. **Minimize damaging fallout.** Creating parallel churches is one of the best steps you can take to minimize any damaging fallout. Keep the experiments off to the side where they will not hurt the existing church if they fail. This approach removes the rocks from the hands of the faithful members of the existing church who may be righteously motivated to view any new practice as a heretical threat. Do everything you can to maintain a firewall between the two so they are unable to negatively impact one another.

How long will this "two parallel churches" season last? As long as is necessary for the reimagined rhythm to be formed. It will likely take at least a year. It could even take three or four. So if you are looking for a quick fix, then leading a church through a process of reimagination is not for you. Once the reimagined rhythms are firmly in place, it will be time to strategically merge the rhythms of the two groups. We will consider how this can be accomplished in an upcoming chapter.

One of the most important components of successfully implementing a reimagination process is leadership. You may have noticed that this transitional phase will require more activated leaders than you think you have right now. Where will they come from? That will be the subject of our next chapter.

Ideate experiments, share results, and compare notes with other church leaders inside the Next Wave Community using the QR code below.

CHAPTER EIGHT

EMPOWER
The Power of Distributed Leadership

The Parable of Pastor Pat

Pastor Pat was really enjoying the reimagine experiments he was involved in. He had joined a martial arts group that met every Monday night. Not only was he discovering new physical vigor, but it dawned on him that he now had more "unchurched" friends than he'd had since high school. He loved the spontaneous conversations that happened at the conclusion of each class. Plus, several of his new friends had invited him to join them for coffee at a local coffee shop near the martial arts studio.

Thursday was his Alpha Night. Pat was having a blast walking through the basics of the Gospel with a group of people who, for the most part, were biblically naïve. He loved their surprising questions and insights. He chuckled at their unintended irreverence and the funny way they pronounced some Bible words.

Pat's wife had embraced the reimagined life by choosing to host a shared neighborhood meal every other Saturday. She cooked up a big pot of stew, baked some fresh bread, and invited anyone who so desired to join Pat's family around the table. They were pleasantly surprised that almost every week, their home was filled with the happy din of neighbors sharing the latest news from around the subdivision.

The initial team of "goers" were finding similar patterns in their lives. They were making new friends, discovering new connections, and enjoying new patterns that put them into regular and meaningful proximity with people who had previously felt far from God. The rhythm of the reimagined church was beginning to take shape. One day, it dawned on Pat that he looked forward to Mondays, Thursdays, and Saturdays but was clearly less excited about the meetings of the existing church on Sundays. He thought to himself, "I have a hard enough time pastoring one church. How in the world am I going to pastor two churches at the same time?"

Delegate, Delegate, Delegate

The subject of delegation deserves an entire chapter because if you don't delegate, you will not successfully reimagine a church. Hard stop. To say it another way, if you try to reimagine a church without enlisting the support of trusted others to whom you can delegate responsibilities, you will fail.

This is a problem because the vast majority of church leaders are not skilled at delegation. They prefer doing it all. They are confident they can do it all faster, better, cleaner, and more completely than anyone else. So they lead comfortably as lone rangers, relishing in the hero status that lonely leadership affords. The well-worn quote "it's lonely at the top" is always in the back of their mind, assuring them that sitting on the lonely church throne is the inevitable plight of the effective pastor.

This serial lack of delegation is a huge reason why the vast majority of churches never serve more than about 150 people and never become reproductive, disciple-making communities. 150 is an organizationally magic number proposed by British anthropologist Robin Dunbar and commonly known as Dunbar's number. Dunbar's number (150) is the maximum number of people that can be connected socially in a personally satisfying way. 150 or less feels like a community where everybody knows your name. 150 increasingly feels like a crowd that one can get lost in. Once the number of people in an organization or group exceeds 150, the group will need to be subdivided in order for the members to maintain a healthy sense of social connection.

One reason most churches serve less than 100 members is because of the way they are led—a lone ranger pastor effectively leading a manageably-sized social group of 150 or less. Most pastors don't delegate because they can lead well without delegating, which is why delegation is not viewed as an essential skill for effective church leadership. Since most churches serve less than 150, lack of delegation is simply not a problem.

However, it is a problem when it comes to leading your church through a process of reimagination. Successful reimagination will require the leader to activate latent skills of delegation. It's not optional. It will probably be a challenge, but it's not impossible. Delegation may come more naturally to some than others, but every leader can learn to delegate. The good news is that a well-executed delegation will empower you to go further, faster no matter what you are trying to accomplish, even in a smaller church that can be successfully led without delegation.

Nevertheless, most church leaders avoid delegation like the plague. Here are some reasons why most leaders prefer doing everything by themselves instead of delegating:

1. **It's easier.** At least it seems easier. Doing everything by yourself means you don't have to spend time finding, preparing, releasing, and overseeing other people.

2. **It's simpler.** Doing is simple. You "just do it." Delegating is inherently complex. When you delegate well, it means you replace the simple act of doing with a new set of responsibilities you may feel ill-equipped to carry out.

3. **It's safer.** Doing it yourself keeps the credit (and the blame) more closely connected to you. You don't have to worry about someone else dropping the ball or doing the job poorly. You avoid the risk of being sabotaged by a well-intended but incompetent volunteer.

4. **It's faster.** At least it seems faster. When you do it, it gets done. Delegation done well slows everything down because it requires you to get others on board, clearly define what you need them to do, activate them as delegees, and monitor their progress.

5. **It's clearer.** Doing it yourself avoids the inevitable lapses in communication. You are talking to yourself. As soon as you involve other people, the potential exists for misunderstandings and other communication failures.

Is delegation really worth it? Here's why the answer to that question is "Yes!"

1. **It's limitless.** Delegation has the potential to exponentially increase the scope of your leadership impact. When competent delegation is built into the fundamental DNA of an organization, the scale of the impact of the organization has limitless potential.

On the other hand, when you do things by yourself, you will inevitably run into the boundaries of your personal capacity. There are not enough hours in the day for you to do everything worth doing by yourself.

2. **It will take you further.** The African Proverb says, "If you want to go fast, go alone. If you want to go far, go together." Yes, doing everything by yourself is faster to begin with, but over time, you will burn out and possibly burn up. The irony of the attribute of delegation is that, over the long haul, not only will you go further but you will ultimately go faster as well. Delegation does slow things down at the start, but once the benefits of delegation begin to accrue, the velocity of a coordinated team will always outpace the best efforts of a lone ranger.

3. **It increases ownership.** Delegation activates and is empowering to others. Doing it alone cultivates a spectator mentality. The ownership dynamic is a real thing. Homeowners have a different perspective than renters. That perspective shows up in the way they care for their living space. Delegation turns renters into owners who will take better care of the cause.

4. **It amplifies your impact.** "I don't want to accomplish anything worthwhile in life," said no leader ever. It's normal for us to want our lives to matter. Delegation is a powerful way to amplify the impact of our lives. Delegation, done well, increases the impact of everyone around us, connecting them to purpose and increasing their ability to be with Jesus on His Mission.

Guidelines for delegating on the reimagination journey.

At the very least, you will need one solid team member. You may be completely unfamiliar with the concept and practice of delegation. You may avoid delegation with every fiber of your being. However, to successfully lead the process of reimagination, you must recruit at least one person to this adventure. You should delegate to this person the key leadership role of the existing church or the key leadership role of the emerging reimagined church. You cannot do both. You can try, but you will fail. It's that simple. It will be best if you can delegate a broad spectrum of tasks to a diverse group of leaders. But to greatly increase the probability of succeeding at the reimagine journey, you will need to identify a trusted delegate to take the lead for one of the two congregations that will exist through the "Transition" phase of the reimagine process.

Use the Eisenhower Matrix to determine what to delegate to others, what to keep, and what to stop doing altogether. This Matrix is a popular planning tool for helping leaders prioritize their to-do list. The origin of the Matrix is attributed to President Dwight Eisenhower quoting J. Roscoe Miller in a speech. "What is important is rarely urgent, and what is urgent is rarely important." Eisenhower used the matrix to solve a common leadership conundrum—the tyranny of the urgent. Too many leaders rush around from one fire to the next, allowing the urgency of their circumstances to set their agenda. Urgency-led decision-making will fatally undermine a reimagination process. Here's how the Matrix can help you delegate well and minimize the tyranny of the urgent.

Begin by listing all of the actions and "to do's" you are responsible for. Divide that list into two segments—tasks only you can do and tasks others can do. Divide the list of tasks only you can do into two more subsets—urgent and non-urgent. Urgent tasks that only you can do should be done as promptly as possible. Non-urgent tasks that only you can do should be calendared, planned for, and built into your future schedule. Urgent tasks that someone else can do should be delegated. Non-urgent tasks that someone else can do should be deleted. Don't allow them to take up brain space or time.

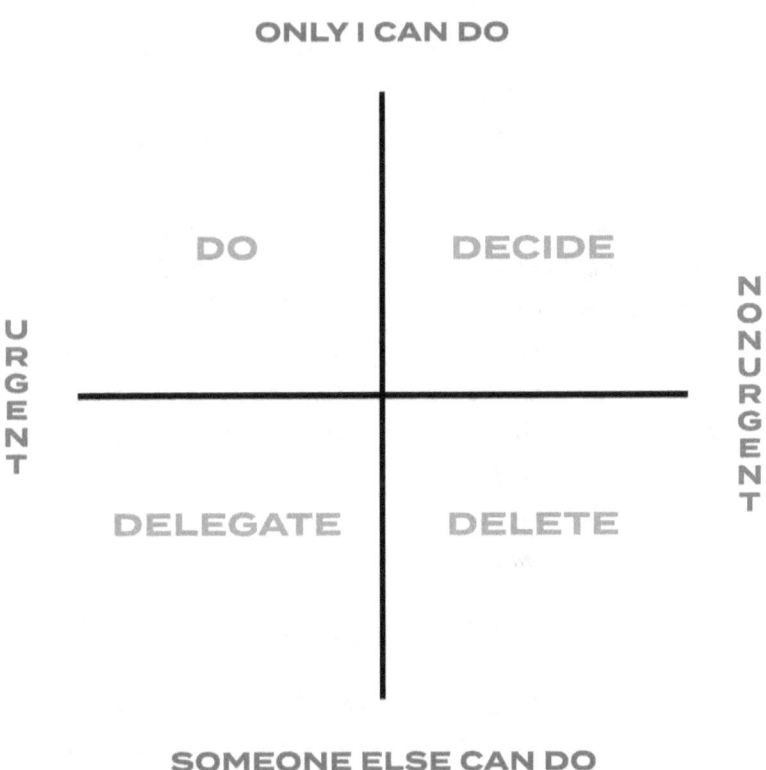

EISENHOWER MATRIX

ONLY I CAN DO

DO   DECIDE

URGENT   NONURGENT

DELEGATE   DELETE

SOMEONE ELSE CAN DO

Use the 70 percent rule—Some leaders get hung up deciding if a task is something only they can do. A helpful guideline is to use the 70 percent rule to determine if you can give the responsibility to someone else. The 70 percent rule states that if someone can do it 70 percent as well as you can, then it is safe to delegate to them. If you don't use the 70 percent rule, you will end up with too many responsibilities on your list of tasks that only you can do.

Yes, delegation is a biblically encouraged practice. Some church leaders hesitate to incorporate what they view as business principles into their church leader habits for fear that they might be watering down the role of God's guidance in the process. Rest assured that delegation is clearly sanctioned and practiced throughout scripture. Moses, who at first glance appears to be the penultimate example of someone who did everything himself, learned to practice strategic delegation.

> *Deuteronomy 1:9-18 – At that time I said to you, "You are too heavy a burden for me to carry alone. The Lord your God has increased your numbers so that today you are as numerous as the stars in the sky. May the Lord, the God of your ancestors, increase you a thousand times and bless you as he has promised! But how can I bear your problems and your burdens and your disputes all by myself? Choose some wise, understanding and respected men from each of your tribes, and I will set them over you."*

> *You answered me, "What you propose to do is good."*

> *So I took the leading men of your tribes, wise and respected men, and appointed them to have authority over you—as commanders of thousands, of hundreds, of fifties and of tens and as tribal officials. And I charged your judges at that time, "Hear the disputes between your people and judge fairly, whether the case is between two Israelites or between an Israelite and a foreigner residing among you. Do not show partiality in judging; hear both small and great alike. Do not*

be afraid of anyone, for judgment belongs to God. Bring me
any case too hard for you, and I will hear it." And at that time
I told you everything you were to do.

Paul the Apostle, another strong leader who may have been prone to do it all himself, strongly endorsed the practice of delegation in his second letter to Timothy.

2 Timothy 2:2 – "And the things you have heard me say in the
presence of many witnesses entrust to reliable people who will
also be qualified to teach others."

Practice solid delegation micro skills. For the aforementioned reasons, few leaders start out as effective delegators. Almost every leader starts out as a "doer." They excel at getting things done and are responsible enough to do it themselves. Leaders who go on to make an impact must learn to move from "doing" to actually "leading." Leaders cast a vision of the preferred future and activate those around them to make that compelling vision of the future a reality. This is the essence of leadership, and it cannot happen without effective delegation. Thankfully, delegation is a skill set that can be learned. Here are some micro-skills every leader can cultivate.

1. **The foundation of effective delegation is trust**. Trust is cultivated over time and experience. Trust does take time (or the enthusiastic recommendation of someone with whom you've already built trust), but once it is formed, trust is an accelerator of everything. Stephen Covey even wrote a book about it called **The Speed of Trust**. Trust lowers the bar of fear that delegated leaders will go rogue and create division in the organization.

Trust greases the skids of accurate communication. Trust softens the impact of mistakes and errors in judgment. Trust simply enables everything to move at a faster pace with less turbulence.

2. **Effective delegation starts with well-executed recruitment.** Healthy teams are invitation-only. Potential team members who invite themselves may harbor motives that will wreak havoc on the reimagination process. The pool of invitees is made up of people the leader trusts and whose behavior is aligned with the trajectory of the reimagined church. Recruitment begins with observation that leads to conversation and, finally, invitation. Observe potential team members through the filter of desired behaviors. For example, if you are looking for a disciple-maker (and you should be!), then be on the lookout for people who naturally make disciples of those around them. When you suspect someone has potential as a team member, engage them in conversation to hear their heart. Listen for alignment with the DNA of the reimagined church. Seek God's guidance, and when you feel confident they will be an asset to the reimagine process, clearly and concisely invite them to join the dream team. The invitation conversation should include carefully clarified expectations and assumptions. What do you expect of them? For how long? What can they expect of you?

3. **Effective delegation results in deployment.** Deployment happens when leaders clearly know what to do, feel empowered to do it, and are actually doing it. You know deployment is happening when good things are occurring. Nothing is more frustrating to highly motivated team members than being invited onto a team and then being left to fend for themselves.

Tell them what you want them to do. If you are unsure of where they can best serve, it is okay to invite them to join you in a journey of discovering where and how they can be best deployed. Successful deployment means they have a clear picture of the scale and scope of their responsibilities. It also means they have a clear understanding of how their progress will be celebrated. The path from recruiting to deployment can be relatively short if you start with people you trust, give them a clear picture of what you want them to do, and then release them to do it.

Memorandum of Understanding

A great tool for increasing the probability that your team member is in alignment with the reimagination path is creating a Memorandum of Understanding. A "Memorandum of Understanding" is the result of a clarification of expectations and assumptions conversation. Ideally, a Memorandum is created by three parties—the two that are seeking alignment and one whose role is to uncover points of misalignment. A sample Memorandum of Understanding is included at the conclusion of this book. You can also find a sample of a Memorandum of Understanding in the Reimagined Church Network Group on the Next Wave Community.)

4. **Effective delegation includes ongoing development**. Inevitably, regardless of how skillfully you recruit and deploy team members, they will say and do things that you wouldn't say and do. This is why it is important to create a culture that

values ongoing growth and development. When the deployed leader makes a poor decision or expresses an opinion that is out of step with the direction of the reimagined church, the result is a great opportunity to strengthen their understanding of what the reimagined church is becoming. If you start with people you trust, you can give them the benefit of the doubt when they go off script. In addition to responding to teaching moments that arise due to errors, ongoing development can be greatly enhanced by regular continuing education moments built into meetings and communication channels.

5. **Effective delegation will result in duplication**. Team members who have a positive delegation experience will understand the benefits and have the knowledge of how to increase their sphere of impact through delegation. In his classic book *Doing Church as Team*, Wayne Cordero introduces the concept of fractals. It's a simple idea that puts the concept of delegation on steroids. When Wayne started New Hope Christian Fellowship, he and his wife invited four carefully chosen couples to assist them in leading the emerging church. He took all of his responsibilities and broke them into four quadrants of responsibility—Leadership development, Stewardship management, Worship, and Missions. He asked each of the couples to take one of the four quadrants, break it into four quadrants, and recruit leaders for each of the four quadrants. And so on, and so on and so on.... 5 couples became 17 couples became 68 couples. The responsibility was continually spread around, with no leader having more than four direct reports. Brilliant. Perhaps a modern-day example of 2 Timothy 2:2 in action.

In case you haven't already noticed, this chapter has been all about delegation. The truth is, we've barely scratched the surface, but you now have a decent framework for setting the power of delegation in motion. It won't hurt to do some more research on delegating well. Delegating is a great example of slowing down to speed up. Initially, it will seem like it is taking longer to achieve your goals, but in the long run, you'll go further faster and the reimagined church will be more robust in every imaginable way!

If you've been following along on this unfolding reimagination journey, you know that we started out with one church and then intentionally turned it into two churches running on different but parallel tracks. To bring the reimagination process to completion, it's time to think about how to bring the two churches back together. Or not. That will be the subject of our next chapter.

Learn how other church leaders have grown their delegation skills. Check out the Next Wave Community by using the QR code below.

CHAPTER NINE

VISIONIZE

Introduce Twenty-First-Century Practices through the Goers

The Parable of Pastor Pat

Pat glanced at the notification on his phone. Another call from Joe Brainard. Joe always made Pat's life more complicated. Pat had been finding creative excuses not to respond for days, but he knew he couldn't put it off forever. He said a prayer and dialed Joe's number.

"Pastor!" Joe's cheery voice belied the strong opinion that Pat knew was headed his way. "Cindy and I would like to take you and Jordan out for dinner to catch up. It's been too long since we just had a good chat!" "Oh boy," Pat thought to himself. "He's pulling our wives into it. This could get complicated."

"Joe," Pat responded out loud. "I've known you long enough to know you've got something on your mind. Jordan and I would love to share a meal with you and Cindy, but I'd rather it would be just fun. What do we need to discuss?"

"Well, Pastor," Joe offered. "I'm concerned. I've been busy with my business lately, so I haven't been able to be as involved with the church as I'd like to be. I've heard rumblings of some changes happening in the way we do ministry. I just want to know first-hand what's going on. I figured the best place to hear about it was straight from you."

"Joe," Pat replied. "I'm grateful for your concern and appreciate that you are reaching out directly to me. The rumblings you've heard about may have something to do with some of the focused ministry groups we've started over the past year. The participants have been really growing in Jesus in ways they never imagined before, and they are really excited to begin sharing what they are learning with other church members. John Stevens is one of them. I know you know John. How about if you, John, and I get together for breakfast one day this week and talk about it?"

Throughout the course of this book, we've been advocating for the parallel church approach to reimagining the church. Our suggestion has been that you literally and deliberately form two parallel churches, leading them at the same time. The idea is that you protect the formation of the reimagined church from the friendly (and not so friendly) resistance of the existing church. Eventually, the time will come when it is right to bring the two parallel churches together—or not.

For the sake of simplicity, we will consider only two options for concluding the parallel church phase of the reimagined church journey. Option one: Skillfully bring the two congregations together. Option two: Continue the existing church and spin off the new parallel church as a separate entity. The truth is, as you navigate through the parallel church phase, you may become aware of other nuanced options that make more sense to you and your leaders. We will consider some of the other options toward the end of this chapter. But to keep our discussion focused, we will assume that the parallel church phase will lead to one of two conclusions—blending or sending.

Bring the Two Churches Together

Blending two churches together is not for the faint of heart. Church mergers are notoriously tricky. Forty years ago, church leadership guru Lyle Schaller said, "Mergers are usually losers." However, more recent studies have indicated that 89 percent of merger efforts experience a favorable outcome.[15] The biggest reason for the huge swing in success is that most modern mergers have a clear leader and a clear follower. This is great news for leaders implementing a process of reimagination because leaders of well-structured reimagination processes have strong leadership influence with both congregations that are preparing to blend.

The key to success in bringing the two congregations together is preparing each congregation for the changes that the blending process will set in motion. Here are some mission-critical preparatory factors for success in merging the two congregations.

1. Careful, clear communication. In the preceding chapter, we discussed the value of creating a Memorandum of Understanding to help define how the two congregations will co-exist amicably. The structure and provisions of the MOU will now be helpful in bringing the two congregations back together. There should be no ambiguity about leadership, governance (how decisions

15   Kyle Rohane and Kevin Miller, Christianity Today Website, "The New Math of Church Mergers," assessed March 1, 2024, https://www.christianitytoday.com/pastors/2019/december-web-exclusives/new-math-of-church-mergers.html

will be made), finances, ministry style, etc. A healthy blending process will include appropriate elements from the original church combined skillfully with the new forms of the reimagined church.

2. Skillful expectation management. Expectations are the root cause of 90 percent of all catastrophic congregational disasters. Ok, I confess. I pulled the 90 percent idea out of the air, but I'm convinced that a comprehensive study would show that 90 percent is close to being right. A good rule of thumb for managing expectations well is summed up in the commonly used maxim "under promise and overdeliver." You may even want to continue to label the coming together of the two congregations as an "experiment." If everyone is expecting an "experiment," they will be comfortable with the inevitable adjustments and mid-course corrections you may need to make as the reimagined congregation takes shape.

3. Authentic relational influence. Deliberately cultivating robust relationships with people and leaders from both congregations is the "oil that greases the skids." The importance of relational connectivity cannot be over emphasized. No matter how carefully crafted your strategic plan is, it is doomed to fail if authentic relationships are not being intentionally cultivated.

4. Aligned leadership. It is crucial that the leader of the existing church publicly demonstrates alignment with and submission to the leader of the emerging reimagined congregation. As mentioned above, one of the main reasons for failed church mergers is typically ambiguity of leadership. Everyone wants

to know who is in charge. Don't allow that question to go unanswered.

5. Cultivate an atmosphere of celebration. The best way to drown out the voices of the naysayers is by amplifying the voices of those who are embracing the reimagined vision for the church, telling great stories of how God is at work in the lives of people who are living out the rhythms of the reimagined community.

With the above preparatory factors in mind, it's time to determine your specific strategy for bringing the congregations together. Merging is definitely a situation where one size does not fit all. However, here are some guiding principles that can be applied to almost every situation.

1. You've got to go down to go up. When tall buildings are built, the workers dig down for what seems like forever so that the building will stand the test of time and the foundation will sustain the weight of the building over time. You are laying the foundation for a new culture. Take the time to get it right! In the merger process, this translates to a lot of time and energy focused on the leaders. It also means you take the time to ensure that the culture of the reimagined church is tangibly established.

2. Keep the contrasts between the existing culture and the new culture clear. The contrast between the existing and reimagined _must be_ crystal clear. Creating a cultural contrast diagram will help remind the leaders of the cultural priorities being fostered in the reimagined church. This clarity will prevent the reimagination effort from being sabotaged by the murkiness of compromise.

Sample Cultural Contrast Diagram

Existing	Reimagined
Status quo	Adaptive
Institutional	Relational
Programs	Lifestyle
Two metrics	Dashboard
Pastor centric	Communitas
Inward focused	Outward focused
Fixed modalities	Fluid modalities

3. Positively prepare both congregations for the process of coming together as one church. At least two months before the actual merger of the churches, proactively begin preparing both congregations to come together around the values of the reimagined church. The existing congregation should be encouraged with stories of the positive missional progress that the reimagined congregation is experiencing. Perhaps a sermon series built around the values of the reimagined church should be preached to the members of the existing church. It should also be made clear to them that the DNA of the existing church will not be the dominant DNA going forward. The reimagined congregation should be reminded that the members of the existing congregation sincerely desire to be part of a church that is an authentic local expression of the Body of Christ. When

possible, they should be encouraged to describe the practices of the reimagined church using the language of the existing church to assist the members of the existing church with the transition. For example, reimagined church members may explain their job fair program as a part of their discipleship/evangelism process.

4. Have a celebration event to signal the transition from two congregations to one reimagined church. The Reimagine Celebration (or whatever you choose to call it) should be highly relational, deliberately optimistic, and different than either the typical gathering of the existing church or the reimagined church. Food should be a big part of the agenda. A dose of appreciation should be expressed for the pioneers who formed the existing church. Prayer and worship should be strongly featured. The new church schedule should be shared in multiple ways. The members of the reimagined church should be encouraged to reach out to members of the existing church and personally invite them to join them for activities that are part of the reimagined rhythm. For example, if the first Tuesday of every month is designated as "Have a Neighbor Over For Dinner" night, an existing church member should be invited to participate in the dinner to see how "Have a Neighbor Over For Dinner" night works.

5. Expect some existing church members to look for a different church. We've devoted an entire chapter to this subject, but it doesn't hurt to repeat it. Good people will leave. Regardless of how carefully you prepare for the transition, some will not be able to handle the change. Treat them kindly as they leave and, in most cases, leave the door open for them to come back.

6. You may find yourself struggling with the changes. The reimagined church will likely have a different set of metrics than the prevailing forms of other churches in the community. Leaders from other churches may privately or publicly question your sanity. "Why would someone blow up a perfectly good church?" they may wonder. Initially, the loss of some long-term members may sting enough to make you question whether you've done the right thing. Stay the course and lean into the values you have been living out during the startup phase of the reimagined church.

A Sample "Coming Together" Story

Part of the inspiration for this book was an appendix I tacked on the end of the book *Next Wave – Discovering the 21st Century Church*." Toward the end of Appendix G in Next Wave, I share the story of a friend who led a church through a reimagination process. I'm sharing this story again here with the hope that this real-life example of a reimagination process will inspire your imagination to envision what a reimagination process might look like in the context where you lead.

> "A friend of mine was assigned by his denomination to take on the challenge of a church near the end of its lifecycle. The church had a decent facility that was paid for. But the congregation had dwindled down to a handful of senior citizens who had neither the vision nor the energy for reformatting the church. After assessing the reality of the situation, my friend decided he had two options. Option 1) Work really hard to inspire his tired little flock to take on the mission of Jesus with renewed vigor. Option 2) Serve the existing congregation as a chaplain and start a new church on the side.

My friend chose Option 2. He kept all of the familiar patterns of the church in place. Every Sunday at 10:45 a.m. (as they had done for decades), the people of the church met for worship. Every Wednesday at 7 p.m., they met for Bible study and prayer. He visited them in the hospital and supported them through weddings and funerals. He devoted about 25 percent of his time and energy into the maintenance side of Option 2.

With the remaining 75 percent of his time and energy, he acted like a church starter. He built relationships with his neighbors, started Alpha Groups for seekers, and hosted Bible studies for saints. None of these activities ever took place at the church building. As the various groups outgrew the homes where they met, they moved into a community center for a Tuesday night Bible study and prayer meeting. Soon, it became clear to everyone that a new community of faith was forming. He began to talk with his community center Bible study group about the possibility of recognizing themselves as a church. They liked the idea.

Meanwhile, back at the existing church, he began a series of messages about forming redemptive relationships with neighbors. He announced that in six weeks, the church would be hosting a "Friend Day" where every member would be encouraged to invite their friends to join them for worship. He asked "Betty" to bake three dozen of her famous chocolate chip cookies. He gave "Fred" a bright orange vest with an equally orange flag on a stick and asked him to direct traffic.

His congregants thought he was a little crazy because they had tried stuff like this before and it hadn't made much of a difference. But he had won their hearts and they decided to play along, hoping that the disappointment wouldn't be too hard on him.

Back at the Bible study at the community center, he announced that he had arranged for a place for them to begin meeting on Sundays. He shared the date for their first meeting, which, of course, just happened to be the date of the Friend Day back at the existing church building. Friend Day arrived. The congregants of the existing church showed up with their trays of baked goods, wondering what they would do with all the leftovers. Fred showed up carrying his orange flag and wearing his orange vest. He dutifully took up his post in the parking lot, feeling a little silly as he prepared to engage in what he expected to be an exercise in futility. But it wasn't long before he rushed into the foyer, announcing to anyone who would listen: "There's a line of cars heading into the parking lot!"

It was on that day that the existing church was reimagined. The newcomers outnumbered the members of the existing congregation ten to one. The old-timers were delighted to once again hear the laughter of children echoing up and down the hallways. Of course, a few of the old-timers expressed frustration over the ways that the newcomers had changed "their" church. But the net result was a dying church received an infusion of life."

Reimagining an existing church IS possible. But it is really, really hard. My friend basically worked two full-time jobs simultaneously to facilitate the reimagining process. This story had a happy ending, but not every reimagining process is blessed with this level of success. With that in mind, it is worth considering the possibility that starting a new church may be the better option. The advantages of starting a new church are many. [16]

The Advantages of Starting a New Church

1. The members of the existing church will not need to disturb their familiar habits and patterns of worship, yet they can celebrate the missional success of the new church they sponsored.

2. The new church can be custom designed for the context and people it's meant to reach and serve.

3. The new church can start with a heavy emphasis on missional engagement from the very beginning.

4. The sending church can be intentional about developing a diversified revenue stream strategy to enable the new church to be sustainable right out of the gate.

5. The new church creates new opportunities and ways for people to lead, serve, and worship.

6. The new church can be started with an embedded DNA of multiplication.

7. Churches that are intentional about multiplication have been shown to be healthier, stronger, and more missionally effective over time.

---

16   Steve Pike, *Next Wave: Discovering the 21st Century Church*, (St. Charles, MO: ArtSpeak Creative, 2022) Appendix G, 264.

I could likely list at least twenty more benefits of starting a new church. It may be wise to consider the possibility that the best way to reimagine your church is to leave the existing church as it is and focus on starting new ones.

How to Know if the Two Churches Should Continue on Different Paths

This book (*The Reimagined Church*) has been written around the concept that the "win" is most members of the existing church making the transition to the reimagined church. However, the best way forward for the two congregations might be that they agree to go separate ways. Instead of coming together, they continue forward as distinct church entities. Here are some markers for knowing when it's right to go separate ways.

1. Key influencers in the existing church are steadfastly refusing to buy into the reimagine process. The current cultural norm of belligerence, born in the crucible of our contemporary political fray, has emboldened some in the church world to import that belligerence into their engagement with the Church. Hiding behind the guise of "standing up for righteousness," the level of ecclesiastical discourse in many church settings has devolved into a form that resembles the mean-spirited mudslinging modeled by their political heroes. Stubbornness and stuckness are mistaken for tenacity and faithfulness. When the posture of the prevailing leaders of the existing church is a resolved resistance to changes that lead to being more aligned with the mission of Jesus, then efforts to help them grow in a healthy direction will likely be unsuccessful.

2. It's clear that the missional effectiveness of the reimagined church will be compromised by the "stuckness" of the existing church. Stuckness means equating staying the same with being faithful to God. People who consistently demonstrate that they equate honoring God with a very narrow set of religious practices will quickly clog up the spiritually vigorous practices of the reimagined church. They will quickly pull it back toward the status quo.

3. The demographic of the newcomers reached by the emerging reimagined church is dramatically distinct from the demographic of the existing church. It will be problematic if the reimagined church rapidly experiences an influx of people who strongly wish to preserve the culture of the existing church. Their legalism will be off-putting and confusing to individuals whose experience with the reimagined church has been refreshing and positive.

When these and other common-sense markers are evident, the better part of wisdom may be to deliberately continue the journey as two distinct congregations.

How to Move Forward as Two Distinct Congregations

1. Clear communication and skillful management of expectations are the pillars of a successful outcome. It is essential that the existing church never be publicly referred to as "stuck" or "dead" or any other negative moniker. It is just as important that the reimagined church not be known as a "church split" or a "rebellion." Over-communicate the positive benefits of having two congregations actively helping distinct types of people

follow Jesus. Both churches are "right." One is not better than the other. These sorts of sentiments need to be communicated in every possible channel in every possible way. Work hard at cultivating alignment between leaders in both congregations.

2. A memorandum of understanding should be developed to help the two churches understand how they will relate to each other going forward. A sample MOU is included in Appendix One at the conclusion of this book.

3. Celebration should be the core posture of the process. Look for every opportunity to express joy and optimism about the emergence of two churches. Even if the hope at the beginning of the reimagined journey was one united church, the fact that the process ends in two distinct churches should not be viewed as a failure.

4. Joint gatherings may be convened to soften the relational impact. In spite of our best efforts to keep the process healthy, people will feel a loss when individuals they love end up in a different worshiping community. Having occasional combined gatherings, especially gatherings of a social nature, will help ease the perceived pain of separation.

Throughout this chapter, we've presented a two-option approach to reimagining your church. The result of following option one is a single reimagined church. The result of following option two is two distinct congregations. This bipolar approach admittedly oversimplifies the potential outcomes of a healthy reimagination process. Your particular reality will be a customized version of the two options influenced by the numerous variables that impact the reimagination process. In some situations, the reimagination process can occur much faster than we have suggested in this book because the existing congregation is in a place where they are ready to welcome radical changes. In other cases, the outcome will be affiliated campuses, not separate stand-alone churches. Nevertheless, factoring in the suggested principles and guidelines will increase the probability of a desirable outcome.

Now that we've arrived at the point where the existing church has been reimagined or a new congregation has been deployed, it's time to think about what happens next. How do we preserve the culture of the reimagined church? We will explore that question and more in the final Section of this book – "Keep Going!"

Whether you're leaning toward blending or sending, the road ahead will almost certainly drain your tank. Join the Next Wave Community using the QR code below to connect with other leaders who will top you off with encouragement.

PART FOUR

KEEP GOING

ONCE THE REIMAGINED CHURCH BECOMES the new norm, it is crucial to develop new habits that will enable the reimagined culture to be sustainable. This final section is all about how to help the reimagined church thrive into the future.

CHAPTER TEN

PATIENCE

Allowing Time for the Leadership Development Process to Gain Momentum

Parable of Pastor Pat

It had been six months since the coming together of the existing and the reimagined congregations. Except for a few minor hiccups, everything was going relatively well. Some of the stauncher members of the existing congregation had chosen to move on to find a church more to their liking. But about two-thirds of the existing church members were doing their best to learn the rhythms and values of the reimagined church. They were able to do so because the benefits of the reimagined church had been clearly demonstrated, and some of them were actively choosing to step into the stream of the reimagined lifestyle. Others kept their arms crossed with a wait-and-see attitude, perhaps hoping that this crazy new rhythm would eventually fade away and things would get back to the good old days they felt more at home in.

The reality of the first six months had made it clear to Pastor Pat what he needed to do to keep the momentum of the reimagined church headed in the right direction. The future of the church depended on a proactive habit of continually identifying, developing, and deploying leaders. Intuitively, Pat knew that cultivating new collective habits into a merged congregation takes time. Ultimately, success in firmly establishing the new habits takes time plus leadership. Ensuring healthy, biblical leadership was the part of that equation Pat could influence the most. But developing leaders had never been his strongest skill. How, he wondered, would he install a robust leadership development habit into the reimagined church?

I'm a sucker for the overnight success story. Did you know that YouTube started out as a dating app? It's true. "Launched on Valentine's Day in 2005, YouTube started as a video dating site with the unofficial slogan "Tune In Hook Up." However, the original idea never gained the traction it sought. The pivotal moment occurred when YouTube's co-founders realized that users preferred to share videos of topics other than dating. Acquired by Google for around $1.65 billion in stock, YouTube users now upload over thirty-five hours of video per minute.[17] The original "dating app" version of YouTube was not successful, and yet there would be no YouTube without the failure of that dating app. We are reminded once again that there is no such thing as a true "overnight" success.

Behind every "overnight" success is the story of long obedience in the same direction. Your dream for the reimagined church might be that it will take off like a rocket headed for the moon. But the reality feels more like a slow boat to an unclear destination. All the good fruit you

---

17 Frances Goh, Collective Campus Website, "5 Overnight Success Stories," accessed March 1, 2024, https://www.collectivecampus.io/blog/5-overnight-success-stories

envisioned is not showing up as fast as you'd hoped. Rarely does anything happen as fast as we'd hoped. When you find yourself wondering if you're stuck in a vision quagmire, it's time to set in motion the reimagined church leaders' secret weapon—patience.

An underlying attitude of patience, tenacity, grit, or whatever you choose to call it will determine the success or failure of the reimagination process. Most leaders can make a lot of noise about change and cast a lot of vision about a better future. But the reimagined church will not emerge overnight. Effective leaders patiently keep nudging the process in the right direction. And they don't do it by themselves.

We've already mentioned the oft-cited proverb, "If you want to go fast, go alone. If you want to go far, go together." I'd like to add an addendum to this proverb: "Patience is better done together." For the reimagined church to go far and for you to have patience that lasts, you will need others committed to journeying with you. In case you haven't yet noticed, one of the themes woven throughout this book is the concept of developing leaders. Leaders, anointed by God's Spirit, are the fuel that moves the Church forward with Jesus on His Mission. No wonder Paul told Timothy to entrust everything to faithful people so they can, in turn, entrust it to others—the well-known 2 Timothy 2:2 principle.

Despite the urgency of establishing a culture that develops leaders, leadership development is a rare practice in far too many churches. The reasons for this unfortunate reality are many. A culprit might be the common practices of ministerial training that are weighted more heavily toward theological concepts than they are on exposing emerging leaders to healthy leadership practices. Another related culprit of our collective low leadership development competency is that emerging leaders have no direct experience with a culture of leadership development. They are equipped with great study habits, sermon preparation concepts, and solid shepherding principles, but robust leadership skills are often treated as an add-on. Paradoxically, at the other end of the spectrum are the pastoral training regimens modeled after business leadership practices. These are focused on developing one's self as a leader not necessarily on developing the leaders around the leader.

The result of this lack of emphasis on the 2 Timothy 2:2 principle is churches whose gospel influence is limited by a serious leadership lid. Whether it's a mega-church built around the charisma of a single, irreplaceable leader or a small group that continues to be a stagnant single cell that never multiplies, the exponential potential of the church is inhibited by a lack of intentionality of developing leaders who empower and equip others to be leaders. The scariest component of this current reality is that a lack of leadership development is considered "normal."

Lack of leadership development may be the reason the vast majority of churches remain small and single-celled, especially in the North American church. Remember Dunbar's number from Chapter Eight? The average leader can effectively lead about 150 people. Most churches tend to max out at the 150 mark and tend to contentedly live out their lives as a comfortable inwardly focused circle and the resulting missional impotence. It does not have to be this way. The Church is rapidly expanding in other parts of the world where leadership development is hard-baked into the DNA.

Leadership Development in the Developing World

Dr. David Garrison has been a student of Islam and God's work among Muslims since his days as an Arabic student in Egypt decades ago. He is the author and editor of nine books on God's work among the world's least-reached peoples. He authored the influential book

Church Planting Movements, which documents the emergence of Jesus Movements in unexpected places across the globe.

Some of the incredible stories shared by Garrison include:

- The story of Ying and Grace Kai, who were the founders of the T4T: Training for Trainers movement, that has resulted in at least two million baptisms and 150 thousand new churches in just one Asian country.

- A Ugandan church planting movement that resulted in the explosion from 300 existing churches to over 3600 in just two years.

- The Bhojpuri Church Planting Movement in an area of India long known as the graveyard of missions and missionaries has resulted in millions coming to faith and tens of thousands of new churches being planted.

- The book *A Wind in the House of Islam* tells the story of how, during the first twelve centuries of the existence of Islam, only three known Jesus Movements occurred that resulted in at least one thousand Muslims moving from Islam to Christ. In the last fifty years, over eighty such movements have taken place.

In addition to a sovereign move of God among these peoples, the catalyst of the movements described above can be attributed to something else. And it is good news for us. In an article on the Church Planting Movement website, Dr. Garrison shares an overview of what we can learn about the crucial role of **leadership development** from the emerging church planting movements around the globe.

"Early in my missionary career, I investigated an emerging Church Planting Movement in West Africa. By the time I was able to interview one of the missionaries at the heart of the movement, the movement itself had already collapsed.

"What happened?" I asked.

"A lack of leadership," he replied. "I was training new leaders as quickly as I could, but the more the movement grew, the farther behind I fell. When I finally went on furlough, the training came to a halt. When I returned to the field, there were only a few churches and leaders still active."

"Because leaders are so indispensable to Church Planting Movements, leadership development that cannot keep up with the movement's exponential growth is certain to lead to its collapse.

There is not one single model for leadership development in Church Planting Movements. However, there are some basic elements *within* these movements that make every leadership training effort much more likely to succeed. These elements include:

- Small, more easily led house churches
- Shared participatory leadership
- Self-feeding from the Bible

When these core elements are in place, leadership becomes bite-sized and manageable, producing a growing number of new leaders for the movement. Once those conditions are met, all kinds of leadership training can accelerate growth. Here are a few that I've come across:

- **Shadow pastoring** – In which a missionary or movement overseer meets privately to offer on-the-job training for emerging church pastors to help answer the questions they face on a weekly basis.

- **Shared leadership** – In many CPMs, churches share leadership to make the task more manageable and to instill mutual accountability and support within the leadership team.
- **Intensive training programs** – Cambodia's movement grew out of transitory "RLTPs" or "Rural Leadership Training Programs." These mobile training programs would take training to the villages where new churches were emerging. Intensive training would last for a few days and then return a few months later with new lessons.
- **Training chains** – One India movement cascaded leadership training from a leader to about twenty trainers who then trained a dozen pastors each, with the result that 240 church leaders received training on a weekly basis.
- **Peer learning** – In parts of China, churches would meet on alternating days so that church leaders could attend other churches to learn from their peers.
- **Training weekends** – Movement overseers, typically non-missionary local leaders, in India and China sometimes scheduled monthly or bimonthly meetings with all of the key house church leaders for a day or a weekend to hear their challenges and offer them just-in-time training.
- **Annual training conferences** – In India's Karnataka and Bhojpuri movements, missionaries sponsored annual events for the training of emerging leaders and church planters.
- **Pastor Study Bibles** – Missionaries have supplemented other leadership development efforts by importing Pastor Study Bibles that are practically seminaries-in-a-book.

- **Distance-based training** – Along with traditional radio and postal correspondence courses, the internet has increased options for distance-based leadership training, particularly in the restricted-access world.

Perhaps you're getting the idea. Church Planting Movements require an ever-growing number of leaders, and there are many ways to meet this challenge.

The best CPM leaders are those who have manageable-sized tasks (i.e., house churches as opposed to mega-churches), mutually accountable co-laborers (as opposed to stand-alone leaders), and self-feeding capabilities (as opposed to dependency on outsiders).

"With these core ingredients in the recipe of the movement, all the other training resources we can provide become icing on the cake. Without these core elements, though, the movement, like a poorly made cake, will likely collapse."[18]

Leadership Development in North America

Lest you think such leadership development intentionality is only effective in a non-American cultural context, I've seen a fantastic example of intentional leadership development firsthand in Hope Chapel, the church planting movement set in motion by Ralph Moore.

While serving as the Lead Pastor of Church on the Terrace in Ogden, Utah, it became clear to me that although the church was healthy by conventional standards, our leadership development practices were

---

18　Church Planting Movements Website, David Garrison, "Leadership in Church Planting Movements," accessed March 1, 2024, https://churchplantingmovements.com/leadership-in-church-planting-movements

weak. Our leadership team began to pray that the Lord would help us discover how to make leadership development an intentional part of everything we did. The Lord sent us Sandy, a leader who had been part of the leadership team at Hope Chapel in Hawaii with Pastor Ralph Moore. She moved to Utah because of her husband's job, and she immediately jumped into the life of Church on the Terrace. She heard about our desire to strengthen our intentionality in developing leaders and offered to help. Long story short, a few months later, our entire leadership team was on a plane headed to Hawaii to hang out with Ralph Moore for a week.

What we saw impacted me deeply and changed the trajectory of our church forever. Hope Chapel was made up of a collection of "Mini-Churches" led by everyday people. The leaders of the Mini Churches got together every other week for fellowship, inspiration, training, and prayer. Through these regular leadership gatherings, the value of leadership development was baked into their leadership template. Discipleship and leadership development were inextricably linked together. When one was happening, so was the other.

Ralph suggested that the best way to understand how leadership development and discipleship worked at Hope Chapel was to participate in a Mini Church and ask them to explain it. And so I found myself seated in a circle in a home on the east side of the island of Oahu. The leader asked me what questions I had.

"How did this group start?" I inquired.

The leader smiled and replied, "A year ago, I was an inmate in a jail about ten miles from here. I came to faith through the jail ministry of Hope Chapel. When I got out of prison, people from the jail ministry told me I needed to join Pastor Ralph's Mini Church so I could understand what should happen next. After being a part of Ralph's Mini Church for a couple of months, I started this group by inviting my friends to be part of it."

I looked at the next person in the circle and asked her to share her story.

"Six months ago, I was an inmate and came to faith through the jail ministry of Hope Chapel. I got out of prison two months ago and just graduated from Pastor Ralph's Mini Church. I plan to be part of this Mini Church for a few months and then gather some of my friends and start a Mini Church for them."

A similar story was shared by the other members of the group. They jokingly referred to themselves as the "Jailbird Mini Church." As I listened in amazement to their stories, it dawned on me—"they don't know any better." They think that what Christians do is help each other follow Jesus and help their pre-Christian friends decide to follow Jesus.

The Hope Chapel rhythm was simple. A weekly corporate gathering (that met in a grade school cafeteria) A weekly Mini-Church experience. Involvement in some sort of intentional outreach habit (jail ministry, etc.) Faithful participation in the leadership development sessions that happened every other week. The leadership development rhythm resembles what David Garrison has seen in Church Planting Movements throughout the world.

- Small, more easily led house churches
- Shared participatory leadership
- Self-feeding from the Bible

The results have been stunning. Hope Chapel has grown virally throughout Hawaii, America, and the world. Here is how Hope Chapel describes itself on its website: "Hope Chapel is a relationship of nearly 2,400 churches born of just twelve people who first met in

1971 in Manhattan Beach, California. The churches thrive on every continent."[19]

Jesus is building His Church, and we are co-laborers with him. A significant characteristic of church planting movements experiencing viral expansion is intentional leadership development. We can't control what Jesus does; we cannot cause miracles to happen; but we can be intentional about developing leaders.

Yeah, but how?

At the beginning of this chapter, I pointed out that intentional leadership development is a rare feature in most churches. The challenge in this reality is that most church leaders have never been intentionally developed themselves, so they tend to develop other leaders the way they have been developed. This means, of course, that they are not intentionally developing the leaders around them! But it doesn't have to be that way. In fact, developing leaders is a central responsibility of spirit-led leadership in the Church that Jesus is building.

If you are one of the rare leaders whose leadership competencies have been honed in the context of an intentional leadership development environment, then make sure you bless the leaders around you with the same rich crucible you were formed in. If you are like most of us (our leadership formation was mostly accidental and unstructured), here are some guidelines for creating a robust and intentional environment of leadership formation.

1. **The best way to learn to lead is to lead.** Always be looking for ways to release the leaders around you into real leadership

---

19   Hope Chapel Website, About page, accessed March 1, 2024, https://hopechapelchurches.com

opportunities. Meaningful leadership opportunities do not need to be expansive or long term to be helpful. Something as simple as assigning your developing leader to set up a room full of chairs can be an important leadership development experience. Observe how they lead (or not). Do they rally and coach others to move the chairs efficiently? Do they bark orders or lead by example? Let them lead, and then give them feedback to increase their leadership competencies.

2. **A coach approach is a powerful method for developing leaders.** The default posture of a coach is to help someone get from where they are to where they want to be. The word "coach" is actually based on the old English word for a vehicle of conveyance. The word picture of what good coaching looks like is of a horse-drawn coach moving a person from one place to another. The coach is the vehicle that takes them to their desired destination. In the case of leadership development, the desired destination is a healthy, well-formed, and active leader. So as the coach, help your developing leader find their way forward as a healthy and complete leader.

3. **Incremental growth is ideal**. "If you are faithful in little things, you will be faithful in large ones. But if you are dishonest in little things, you won't be honest with greater responsibilities" (Luke 16:10 NLT). A common leadership development error is giving a developing leader too much responsibility too quickly. Deliberately ratchet up their level of responsibility incrementally so they can prove themselves faithful in the small things first. If they balk at doing the small things, they should not be entrusted with the big things.

4. **Highly relational cadres of leaders create a healthy environment for growth.** Leaders learning together in a learning community is much more powerful than individuals learning alone. Whatever form your leadership formation process takes, it should include environments that allow developing leaders to learn from each other in real time. Read books together and talk about them. Enjoy experiences together (sky diving, anyone?) Learn in groups as much as possible.

Four Essential Leadership Development Components

Your leadership development process will best be formatted to fit the specific culture of your situation. However, whatever shape your leadership development process takes, it will need to have the following minimum components:

Discover – Where do the leaders who need to be developed come from? Finding leaders to develop should not be left to chance. A crucial part of your leadership development strategy will be a plan for discovering the potential leaders who are already present in your organization. This discovery component must not be left to chance. Otherwise, your entire leadership development pipeline will be bogged down waiting for individuals who think they are leaders to raise their hand and ask to be developed (or simply declare themselves leaders and potentially start wreaking havoc on the church).

Develop – Once potential leaders are discovered, have in place a clear pathway for them to cultivate and enhance their leadership skills. Your framework or curriculum for developing leaders should be selected based on your context and access to leadership development resources. Thankfully, there are a multitude of Biblical worldview-based leadership development tools/programs to choose from. Some that immediately come to mind are Maxwell Leadership (maxwellleadership.com), Patrick Lencioni's The Table Group (tablegroup.com), and The Anser Group's Essential Leadership (tag.coach). What's most important is to be intentional about embedding leadership development into the fabric of the reimagined church.

Deploy – Even though actual leadership experiences will be part of the develop phase, it's important that those you develop are eventually deployed into key leadership roles so that their leadership gifts may benefit the church. Creating a line of demarcation between the development phase and being assigned a clear leadership role is important. Public acknowledgment and/or some type of commissioning moment will help everyone in the organization recognize the value of making themselves available to be deployed as a leader. The key here is to minimize the number of individuals who become "professional leadership students" but never move on to actually be activated as leaders in God's Church.

Duplicate – A part of every robust leadership development process will be embedding the culture of leaders producing leaders. Ultimately, every leader should consider it normal to be discovering, developing, deploying, and duplicating new leaders.

The purpose of this chapter has been to acknowledge the crucial need to be intentional about the formation of leaders within the organization. Constant leadership development will go a long way to ensuring that the forward momentum of the reimagined church's mission will not stall due to a lack of catalytic leaders. However, the lack of leaders is not the only threat to the ongoing progress of the reimagined church. Every reimagined church has a hidden enemy that must be effectively dealt with. Otherwise, it will silently sabotage the reimagined church. That enemy will be the topic of our next chapter.

Get tips and insights for leadership development inside the Next Wave Community.

CHAPTER ELEVEN

STEADY

Overcoming the Muscle Memory of Religious Habits

The Parable of Pastor Pat

The transition was complete. The unhelpful habits of the existing church were now just a memory. On the surface, it felt like the reimagined way of being the church had become the new normal. Sort of. Occasionally, Pat found himself daydreaming about drifting back into the old comfortable habits. He wasn't the only one.

Sister Stephens's phone number lit up on his phone. Before he thought about it, he answered. Without any warning, Sister Stephens let him have it. "You killed our church, Pastor. It will never be the same. I want you to know that for the first time in my life, I'm thinking about looking for another place to worship where they take church seriously." She paused to take a breath. "Are you listening to me?" she demanded.

"I do hear you. I mean it. I miss our Wednesday night Bible Study in the fellowship hall. I loved getting together with everyone just to study God's Word. Those were precious times,

and so much easier to prepare when I did all the teaching. Now that we are having open-ended discussion times with our neighbors, it's much harder to prepare because no matter how hard I try, I never do a good job of guessing what people will say."

"Then why do you keep doing it," she wondered out loud.

"Because the Lord led us in this direction, and we are seeing so much more missional fruit than we've experienced ever before. Last month, we baptized twenty-six new believers. That's more than we used to baptize in a year!

"Old habits die hard." The origin of that phrase is a little murky. Some believe that Benjamin Franklin first said it in a speech. Others say it emerged as a common English phrase in the thirteenth century. But everyone agrees it is painfully true.

The longer a church has lived, the more fixed its congregational habits will be. And they will die hard. Harder than hard. In an article in *Psychology Today*, Shahram Heshmat explains that the reason old habits die hard is due to what he calls "unconscious motives."[20] In other words, we are motivated by motives that we are not consciously aware of. Why does a certain song make me weep? Why do I like to always sit in the same place? Why do I feel closer to God in a particular setting? Heshmat would say the answer to each of these questions lies in the unconscious recesses of our brains. We feel strongly about something, but we don't know why. We believe something is right, but the reason we think it is

20 Sharam Heshmat, "Why Old Habits Die Hard," Psychology Today Website, February 16, 2016, https://www.psychologytoday.com/us/blog/science-choice/201602/why-old-habits-die-hard

right is difficult to articulate. We feel before we think. We decide before we ponder. "That cookie I just ate tasted so good!" "Oh, wait a minute, I've decided to be on a diet and that cookie is not included. Why did I eat it?"

Habits are formed by repeated actions that create neuronal pathways in the brain. The longer the actions are repeated, the more ingrained the habit becomes. Once a habit is ingrained in the brain (literally a neuronal pathway embedded in the brain), it takes a lot of work to break the habit. The difficulty is compounded when the habit is shared by a group of individuals whose repeated actions have reinforced the same habit in each individual. It then becomes a collective habit that is reinforced by the added force of peer pressure.

So how are congregational habits modified? Heshmet suggests that "reflective awareness" leads to free will. Reflective awareness refers to the act of intentionally becoming aware of the habits shaping our lives. But just being aware of the habits is only the beginning of changing them. Habits are formed through repeated actions and can be changed through repeated actions. Forming habits takes time, so it should be no surprise to us that it will take time for new ones to form.

Therein lies the challenge. The fact that the church has carefully and strategically transitioned to a new set of collective habits does not necessarily mean that the new habits are firmly affixed in the core DNA of the church. Heshmet, referring to helping a person change their habits, observes that "rapid symptom relief is not permanent."[21] In other words, the fact that someone has changed their habits in the short term

21   Shahram Heshmat Ph.D., "Why Old Habits Die Hard," Psychology Today, February 1, 2016, https://www.psychologytoday.com/us/blog/science-choice/201602/why-old-habits-die-hard

does not mean they have changed their habits in the long term. The same reality is painfully true for a collective of individuals who make up a congregation. It will take time for the new habits to settle in and become the new norm. The new habits can become permanent, but it will take time.

How do you nurture the new habits so that they become a permanent aspect of the core DNA of the church?

- Invite the original dream team members to constantly lead by example. Your original dream team members hold the key to embedding the new habits into the DNA of the reimagined church. They've helped form the habits. They've been living them out the longest. They are the best equipped to embody the new habits in a way that everyone can see and be inspired by. Your best time and most focused energy should be reserved for the members of your original dream team. When they catch the vision, they will multiply it in ways you never could. A greater spectrum of church members will be inspired to aspire to live out the emerging habits of the reimagined church.

- Have pastoral one-on-ones with people who are clearly struggling with the new church rhythms and coach them toward change or give them your blessing to find another place to worship. I realize that in the previous nurturing suggestion, I recommended that you give your best and most focused time to your original dream team members. However, you will need to connect directly with people in the church who are struggling mightily with the new ways of being and doing Church. It is mission-critical that you help them find a healthy way forward. When you become aware that a member is struggling to adopt the habits of the reimagined church, you basically have three options for how to respond.

Option one is to ignore them. That one never works out well for them or for the church. Even though it is an option, it's not really an option. Leaving disgruntled folks to fester in their discontent will only lead to problems for everyone down the line.

Option two is to coach them through to change. It's possible that with patience and tenacity, this might actually happen. However, as we've already noted in this book, change is really hard for people. It is worth a try, but if they are not reasonably responsive to your efforts at coaching them through change, then it is likely time to move on to the next option.

Option three is to help them find another church—a church where they can flourish. Seriously. Except for very rare examples, most communities will have healthy church options for your unhappy members to choose from. This is actually a great opportunity to remind them and to remind yourself that the reimagined church is "A" way to be the Church, not "THE" way. Of course, you need to really believe this yourself to ensure the authenticity of your efforts to help them find another worshipping community. A great way to be prepared to help someone transition is to be familiar with the missional culture of the other churches in your community. Get to know their leaders; get to know what they care about deeply; and then help your disillusioned members make the shift. Introduce them to your pastor friend at the other church. Talk up the attributes of the church that are a good match for the desired worshipping context of your departing member.

- Frequently remind everyone of the "why" behind the new habits and practices. Every chance you get, remind everyone why you are doing everything—especially the new habits you are hoping will become second nature to the members of the church. Build a "why" moment into every public gathering. Some reminder of the "why" should be included in every email, newsletter article, or congregational communication that you send out. This is important because when the "why" becomes disconnected from the "what," the new "what" will be replaced with the old "what" and you'll end up right back where you started.

- Celebrate the outcomes of the new habits through story sharing. Tell stories. Tell stories way more often than you lay down carefully constructed theological arguments. Stories empower people to see the new habits lived out in real life. It's easier to imitate new habits than it is to unearth them from theological discourse. Seeing is believing, and robust believing leads to doing. In an article in *Harvard Business Review*, Vanessa Boris reminds us why storytelling is so effective for learning. Besides enumerating some other great benefits, she reminds us that storytelling works with all types of learners—40 percent of learners are visual; 40 percent are auditory; 20 percent are kinesthetic. Stories allow each learner type to "get the point" in a way that is best for them.[22] It's good to support new habits with pithy slogans, mottos, and value and vision statements. But well-told stories are a crucial tool in your efforts to embed the new habits into the everyday practices of the people you are leading.

- Don't give in to the thought that everyone must be tired of hearing about the reimagined process—that's when they might be hearing it for the first time! Every leader has found this to be true. We grow tired of hearing ourselves say the same thing over and over again. Our spouse is tired of hearing it over and over again. However, the conveyance of new thought patterns requires repetition, so it's important to keep beating the drum, ringing the bell, or (insert your favorite "sound the alarm" metaphor here). However, repeating the same thing over and over does not necessarily mean using the same words. In fact, being creative about saying the same thing is essential. Invite your dream team into regular brainstorming sessions where you discover together how to say the same thing in different ways. Also, varying the communication mode is important

---

22 Vanessa Boris, "What Makes Storytelling So Effective For Learning," Harvard Business Review Website, Posted December 20, 2017, https://www.harvardbusiness.org/what-makes-storytelling-so-effective-for-learning/

to ensure that the various learner types are being well-served. Depending on what expert you are consulting, there are at least three and perhaps ten or more learning types. If your communication mode only connects with one learning type, you will struggle to inspire excitement about the reimagined church.

- Time is on your side. Consistency over time will help the new habits to become embedded in the ethos of the church. My mentor, Dr. George O. Wood, used to describe leading with these words: "plod on, plod on, plod on." I think he was trying to remind us that exercising leadership is playing the long game. We want to throw a spectacular "hail Mary" touchdown pass, but those plays are rare. In 2022, the BEST team in the NFL gained an average of 6.5 yards per play. Most plays are unspectacular. In the same way, most leadership "plays" are just doing the right thing for the right reason over and over and over again. The longer you consistently reinforce the new ethos of the reimagined church, the more buy-in you will receive from congregation members.

- Avoid habit creep—no compromise! Watch for signs that the old habits are seeping back into the life of the church. For example: Old habit= doing every church activity at the church building. New habit= prioritizing using the building as an event center, which means that church activities need to share or even give preference to building use that strengthens the relationship with the community. Habit creep would mean that church activities begin to replace community activities, and over time, the church becomes increasingly isolated from the greater community. Effective leaders of healthy reimagined churches will be vigilant about recognizing little decisions that might potentially move the church away from the reimagined path.

- Resonate with their sense of loss. There will be days when you yourself will miss the old habits. Having grown up in a church that prioritized lots of church meetings as important for spiritual formation, I sometimes miss the comfort of receiving regular doses of Bible knowledge carefully prepared for me by someone else. The reimagined church that I'm part of believes that proactive engagement in the mission of Jesus takes priority over sitting passively on the receiving end of someone else's exegesis of scripture. Yes, we do have teaching moments, but I find my reimagined church creates more space for me to live out the Bible insights I gain. The rhythm of the reimagined church makes me more of a participant than a spectator. In the increasingly complex culture we all share, I do find myself having fond memories of simpler times when all that was expected of me was to show up and take notes. Be sure to exercise grace and empathize with your congregants who mourn the loss of the church they grew up in.

What if you suspect you are "beating a dead horse?"

This book has been written with the assumption that you as a leader are hoping to help the church you lead transition from a familiar but increasingly missionally impotent format to a reimagined local church optimized to be with Jesus on His mission of seeking and saving the lost. We've suggested that the better part of wisdom involves setting in motion a new church culture alongside the existing one and then, once the new church culture is formed and has adequate momentum, bringing the new culture into the existing one, resulting in a transformed church that is more faithfully with Jesus on His mission.

As we wrap up this chapter on staying steady and not wavering, we should consider the possibility that despite your best efforts to lead your church through the transformation from existing to reimagined, you suspect that the culture of the existing church is too firmly entrenched for ANY change process to be effective. How do you know when it is time to stop beating the proverbial "dead horse?"

- Seek feedback from your key leaders. Deciding to give up on a reimagination process should never be a decision made in isolation. It's especially wise to solicit input from the dream team members who have been in the change process the longest. Use a SWOT (Strengths, Weaknesses, Opportunities, Threats) to invite input into the status of the reimagined transition. If this group determines together that the collective buy-in of existing church members has not reached critical mass (10–20 percent), then it might be time to take your foot off the reimagination gas pedal. Based on the feedback from your leaders, rate the health of your reimagination process with a number from 1–10, with 1 being very poor and 10 being optimal.

- Monitor the behaviors of your members. The old axiom that says "actions speak louder than words" is so true. Long-time members of North American church culture have been conditioned to avoid any perception of disagreement. Many American Christians mistake verbal agreement with behavioral buy-in. They don't want to be accused of being divisive, so they nod their heads in agreement with everything they hear, even with ideas they have no intention of putting into practice. Wise church leaders will look past the verbal and even physical signs of affirmation and instead watch the behavior of their followers very carefully. Are they living the lifestyle that the reimagined church embraces? If so, fantastic. If not, then it's time to ask what's really going on here? Behaviors mean more than heads nodding in agreement. Based on your observation of the behaviors of your members, rate the overall health of the explicit buy-in level of your congregants—1 being no buy-in and 10 being the best possible level of buy-in.

- Run your expectations through a reality check. Unrealized expectations are a huge contributor to failed reimagination processes in churches. Leaders are not immune to expectations that are out of alignment with reality. In fact, the most optimistic leaders are prone to expecting transformation to happen way too fast. Expecting the entire church body to pivot without any hiccups is not a realistic expectation. Be cautious about abandoning a reimagination process because of an artificially imposed timeline. However, when you've been careful about keeping your expectations aligned with reality and the reimagined church is not truly emerging, it could be time to consider discontinuing your efforts to reimagine the church and become intentional about helping the preexisting culture of the existing church become the best version of itself. Based on your careful analysis of your expectations for the implementation values and practices of the reimagined church, rate the current state of expectational alignment with reality—1 being completely out of alignment and 10 being perfectly aligned.

Rate each factor above, add up your numbers, and divide by three. The result will help you decide whether it's time to discontinue the reimagination process. If the number from the above process is 7 or above, then it's time to keep pressing forward with the reimagination process. A total of 4–6 indicates that further prayer and evaluation is needed to determine how to best proceed. A number of 3 or below means it is likely time to discontinue the reimagination effort. The existing congregation is just too stuck for you to lead them through a change process.

What to Do if Your Number Is 3 or Below

It's possible that when all is said and done, you might need to contemplate a future that does not include your vision of a reimagined church made up of the existing church and the newly discovered reimagined church. Now what? At least two options stand out:

- Option one – Determine if planting a church or starting a new site is the right outcome. As we've already shared, there are many benefits to this approach.
    - It allows the existing church to rapidly resume business as usual.
    - It protects the efforts of the dream team from being viewed as wasted.
    - It allows the existing church to celebrate the accomplishment of incubating a missionally effective church.
    - It allows the dream team to accelerate the missional momentum of the reimagined church without going through a complex process of integrating back into the existing church.

- Option two –Develop a transition plan back to a modified "business as usual" culture. Assuming you choose not to start a new church, then the next best option is to integrate the dream team back into the existing church in a healthy way. Following are some keys to success in moving forward with a modified business-as-usual strategy:
  - ○ Remind everyone this was an experiment.
  - ○ Celebrate lessons learned.
  - ○ Incorporate what you can from the learned lessons back into the normal rhythm of the church.
  - ○ Take your time. Avoid sudden moves that scare people off.

At this point in the process, you are experiencing one of at least three possible outcomes to the reimagined church journey:

One: You have successfully developed a reimagined church, and the new rhythms of that church are fully integrated into the normal life of the existing church. For all practical purposes, the existing church has now become the reimagined church.

Two: You have realized the best way forward is for two different churches to emerge from this process—a reimagined one and an existing one.

Three: The experiment of forming a reimagined church has ended without success, and the existing church has returned to her normal rhythms of being the church.

But we aren't quite ready to conclude this book. There are two more factors we must consider before our reimagined church thought process is complete: *Metrics and models*. Keep reading...

We have leaders in the middle of their reimagining experiments right now inside the Next Wave Community. Join the Community today using the QR code below to hear their stories.

CHAPTER TWELVE

CELEBRATE
Measure What Matters

The Parable of Pastor Pat

At the beginning of his reimagine journey, Pastor Pat felt like a lone voice crying in the wilderness. So many of his ministry peers were content to do their best with church as usual. Pat had a hard time seeing how that would end well, so he leaned into the reimagine journey, content to go it alone.

But a funny thing happened along the way. He discovered other leaders who were themselves on a journey of reimagination. One such leader was Pastor Bob, who led what Pat thought was a thriving church from a different denomination on the other side of town.

Pat connected with Bob at a city-wide minister's fellowship meeting when they randomly ended up at the same table. The speaker that day was a veteran church consultant who urged the ministry leaders to stay the course and stick with tried-and-true ministry strategies. Pat was frustrated by the advice of the expert. During a brief "get to know your neighbor" break in the program, Pat introduced himself to Bob and asked him what he thought of the speaker's insights.

"I disagree," Bob replied. "Staying the course is the best way I know to guarantee that the church I lead will not survive over the next decade."

Pat was shocked by his frank assessment. "Why do you say that?" he inquired.

"Well," Bob mused. "I've been leading my church through a process of rediscovering how we can effectively be with Jesus on His Mission. We've gone back to some basics that we realized had been lost along the way. We're beginning to see some exciting fruit from our efforts. We've exited the treadmill of maintaining the institutional status quo and started climbing the mountain of missional adventure. We are having a blast!"

Pat almost couldn't contain his joy in finding a kindred spirit.

"I think our church might be doing the same thing!" he replied. Let's compare notes and see what we can learn from each other."

Like Pastor Pat, you are not alone and you are not crazy. If you've been wondering if others are leading their church through a process of reimagination, the answer is yes" God saw this coming, and he's been prompting the leaders of His church to move toward a diversity of missionally effective ways of being the church. In fact, so many of these emerging "reimagined churches" exist that it is possible to see different genres beginning to come into focus.

This book has deliberately stayed away from presenting any "models" of church. Our hope is that the processes described in the book will result in each leader hearing from God in a fresh way. Models are not bad, but using a model as a guiding principle can be problematic. Too many leaders fall in love with a model and then try to impose it on a context. Sometimes the model fits the context, but too often, it is an awkward fit, resulting in wasted time, energy, and resources.

The effective use of models starts with a deep evaluation of guiding principles and contextual exegesis. With the principles and context clearly in mind, a proven model can provide a framework to move the emerging church from concept to reality. "Proven" is a keyword in that last sentence. It means there is evidence that a specific ministry approach is helpful in a given context.

A model is more likely to be helpful when there is a high degree of similarity between the context where the model has been tried and found helpful and the context where the model may potentially be used as a guide. For example, a model that works well in a suburban community in the deep South may not be a helpful guide in the heart of urban Boston. If only understanding context were as simple as such an obvious example. In real life, context is a multi-faceted concept that includes at least the following elements:

- **The background, experience, and preferences of the church starter.** Every church starter comes to the season of starting a new church with a history of religious heritage, educational background, family of origin issues, life stage impacts, etc. All of these will influence the willingness and ability of the starter to implement various models and thrive in various cultural contexts.

- **The specific history of the locality.** Every locality has a general history that will impact the relevance of a given model. For example, when I planted a church in Utah, I initially downplayed the need to acquire a building of our own. But as we became more familiar with Utah's cultural values, we realized that owning our building was an important part of the missional success equation in that context.

- **The religious history of the locality.** The model you choose should also be influenced by the reality of the religious history of the place. Localities where the general attitude is hostile to the Church will benefit from a different guiding model than in places where the Church is still considered a community asset.
- **The micro-culture of the locality.** Micro-culture refers to the very immediate geographic culture where the church serves. In city environs, it will likely be the culture of the neighborhood. In suburban places, it might be the culture of the subdivision. Rural small towns form their own micro-cultures. The micro-culture should definitely be factored into the process of adopting a guiding model.
- **The larger culture of the region surrounding the locality.** Think about the general differences between people who live in the Northwest US and people who live in the Southeast US. One region tends to be more progressive. One tends to be more conservative. Again, this should be factored into your consideration of a guiding model.
- **The national cultural influence on the locality.** The overarching culture of the country will also be a factor. A local Russian church will likely need to be informed by a different model than a local American church.

If the above designations sound like common sense to you, that should come as no surprise. They are simply reasonable lenses through which the discovery of an appropriate model should be processed. I'm constantly surprised by how many smart leaders overlook these common sense notions because they are personally enamored with a model that they favor. Too often, they are distracted by the encouraging outcomes of the model and choose to uncritically apply the model to their context without serious consideration of its cultural fit. The shoulders of the ecclesiastical highway are littered with the dead hulks of broken-down churches that were blindly guided by an attractive model alone.

You get the point. Start with the context and then look for a guiding model that fits that context. Resist the urge to reverse that order. It will be a choice you will live to regret.

With that "model" warning in mind, we can now safely introduce some "models" thinking for our consideration. The following list is not exhaustive, and the models described are not perfect. These are simply examples of different ways the Church is adapting to specific contexts. Please don't just cherry pick a model; google the website and decide whether this is the model for you. Take your time. Ask God for wisdom. It is very possible that your context will not be served well by ANY of these models. In that case, you will need to create your own model by patiently listening to the Holy Spirit, asking the right questions, and courageously trying things you've never done before.

Models of Reimagined Churches

Dinner Church – Verlon Fosner is the pioneer and founder of the modern-day expression of gathering the church around a meal. The Dinner Church model emerged out of a conventional church that recognized it was increasingly out of sync with the changing neighborhood. Verlon began to deeply study the history of the early church and discovered that it was very common for the earliest expressions of the Church to have a shared meal at the center of their time together. The modern-day dinner church approach was first utilized in the first ring neighborhoods surrounding Seattle's Central Business District. It has now been adapted and utilized in a variety of contexts across the nation and around the world. You can learn more here: dinnerchurch.com.

Hybrid Micro/Celebration – Matthew and Elora Collver grew up in the South and cut their ecclesiastical teeth on the pews of conventional church expressions that tended to take the church to the already convinced. Hungering to faithfully join Jesus on His mission to seek and save the lost, they joined a missional team that moved into Summit County, Colorado, and formed a house church movement intended to reach people far from God in a context that is unquestionably spiritually challenging. In 2015, they followed the prompting of the Spirit to start a new church in a marginalized neighborhood in urban Denver, Colorado. The culture of the neighborhood led them to develop the "Hybrid Micro/Celebration" model that draws on the best of the historic church of the past, the conventional church of the twentieth century, and the emerging church of the twenty-first century. A key feature of this model is that the church alternates between large gatherings and micro churches every other week. Learn more at thehillsdenver.com.

Co-Working Church/Dance Church – In 2015, Jose and Jenna Perez sensed God's calling to start a new church in an urban Minneapolis neighborhood. At that time, Jose was serving on the staff of a conventional church in Duluth, Minnesota. As he contemplated the challenge of starting a new church in the city, a huge question for him was, "How will this church be financially sustainable?" As he prayed about the financial challenge, he began to realize that the answer to the question might be in his occupation before becoming a pastor—Jose had been a professional dancer and had started numerous dance studios across the nation of Venezuela. He realized that people in the urban neighborhood might patronize a dance studio before they chose to attend a church. He and Jenna worked together to start "One Reason Dance Studio" first and then opened "One Reason Church." Basically, the dance studio pays for the building and the church supports pastors Jose and Jenna. This is a fantastic example of the increasingly popular "Co-vocational" model in action. Check out the latest on their adventure at onereasonchurch.com and onereasondance.com.

Neighborhood Focused – As staff members of a conventional church in a different part of New York City, Eric and Sarah Hoke had little time to interact with their immediate Bronx neighbors. They began to wonder what it would look like to start a neighborhood-focused church that existed to deliberately help their neighbors find and follow Jesus. All Saints Church was born through a hyper-lean startup process and continues to thrive to this day. Despite the fact that the weekly attendance at All Saints hovers in the forties, they've helped start other neighborhood-focused churches in other neighborhoods in NYC. Check it out at allsaintsnyc.com.

Virtual Church – Chestly Lunday and Jeff Reed are the co-founders of the Digital Church Network. This is a growing community of churches and church leaders exploring the emerging frontier of creating a digital church. In the latter part of the twentieth century, every church that hoped to continue to be with Jesus on His mission created a website. In these early years of the twenty-first century, every church must have a digital expression of itself. Jeff and Chestly are bringing together digital pioneers to accelerate the emergence of virtual expressions of the church everywhere. Learn more at fam.digitalchurch.network/feed.

Missional Communities – Hugh and Cheryl Halter had a special needs child whose physical challenges prevented them from being part of a conventional church. Rather than feeling isolated from the Church, they decided to be the church in their own home and invite their nearby neighbors to join them in following Jesus. That idea not only met their needs for connecting to the Church but has resulted in a multitude of fresh and innovative ways to be a thriving church faithfully in the context of the surrounding community. You can learn more at hughhalter.com.

Decentralized Micro Church Network – In 2019, about eighties followers of Jesus left the structures of the prevailing church to become a grassroots movement in Kansas City, MO. Their forty-year dream is to see the emergence of 21,000 micro churches connecting with twenty-one hubs. This dream is guided by eighteen values that reflect their theological convictions. Rob Wegner serves as the key visionary for what is now known as the KC Underground. This model is now being adapted in communities all across the US. Here's where you can find out more: kcunderground.org.

Artesian Multi Site – Steve Milazzo is the lead pastor of a strong, conventional model church in Valley Stream, New York. Steve and his leadership team have been innovating the "multisite" approach by starting neighborhood-focused congregations that take the best from the sending church and appropriately incorporate cultural elements from the neighborhood. The result is that each multi-site campus feels like it was built by and for the neighborhood. At the same time, the local multi-site benefits from the sharable elements of the sending campus, such as worship leaders, children's ministry personnel, etc. You can learn more about this emerging model here: bethlehemag.org.

Hub and Spoke Network – Lucas Pulley is the Executive Director of the Tampa Underground. This model was birthed out of a year of direct exposure to and careful observation of a church planting movement in the Philippines. The original leaders (led by Brian Sanders) returned to Tampa and adapted what they had learned to the context of Tampa. The Underground is now a "Hub and Spoke" Network of hundreds of missional expressions linked together by some basic theological foundation themes and commonly held values. The missional expressions all carry out what they do at their own discretion and cooperate together for commodity functions like administrative support, bookkeeping, etc. This model could be a great template for a permission-giving large church to send out custom-built expressions into the nooks and crannies of culture and community.

Community Focused – Bryce Baldwin became the pastor of a 115-year-old church in upstate New York. As he got to know the church and the community, two realities became clear:

1. The church was not well connected to the community.
2. Joblessness was a felt need in the community.

He discovered that there was only one job fair option serving the neighborhood, so he decided to rally the church around the idea of hosting a community job fair. Now, job fairs are a regular ministry focus of the church. The principle Bryce tapped into was to simply find a community challenge/opportunity and then find a way to solve the challenge or step into the opportunity. You can learn more about the Community Focused model by joining the Better Place Network in Next Wave Community.

Although the above models look different on the surface, they are built on a set of similar values that seem to be present in every reimagined church:

- **A foundation of disciple-making.** Every emerging model
  described above places a premium on disciple-making as
  THE primary identity of the church. While all of them
  have some sort of regular gathering habit as a part of the
  church's rhythm, they have all moved away from viewing
  "going to church" as the key church focus. "Being sent out
  to make disciples" has replaced "going to church" as the
  crucial metric that indicates missional progress. "How many
  disciples are being made?" is an equally and perhaps even
  more important question to them than "how many people
  attended the Sunday worship gathering?" Additionally, they
  all have expanded their understanding of what it means
  to be engaged in making a disciple. They are deliberately
  joining Jesus on His mission to seek and save the lost. They
  view disciple-making as any action that helps a person move
  toward Jesus and/or grow in Jesus.

- **A sustainable financial strategy.** In case you haven't
  noticed, the Church is in the midst of an economic
  revolution. An increasing number of church leaders
  recognize that the prevailing economic strategies for
  funding the ongoing ministries of the church are not
  adequate for the challenges of twenty-first-century culture.
  Specifically, the idea that "self-sustaining" means all the
  costs of operating the church are funded by the tithes and
  offerings of the parishioners is increasingly unrealistic. In
  Chapter Three of *Next Wave*, we suggest that churches that
  thrive in the twenty-first century will shift from seeking
  to be "self-sustaining" to being "sustainable." Sustainable
  means that other revenue streams besides tithes and

offerings become part of the financial sustainability strategy of the church. For example, micro churches, meeting in homes/restaurants/bars, etc., and led by leaders employed in the marketplace do not require the same funding strategy as "brick and mortar" churches that own a building and have a full-time paid staff. Sustainable funding approaches mean that, whatever the form of the church, it is sustainable. All of the models above are financially viable due to a non-traditional (but legal and ethical) approach to funding.

- **An organizational structure that honors missional innovation.** Each of the models above exists because the leaders did not feel constrained by the need to "do church the way it's always been done." Instead, they have allowed the cultural context to appropriately shape the way they live out and proclaim the gospel. Typically, they start with a question like "how are disciples best made in this context?" and then build their organizational structures around the answer to that question. The KC Underground story is a great example of missional innovation driven by the pursuit of holistic discipleship well-done.

- **A set of metrics to measure missional progress.** It's been implied already, but we need to clearly declare that new models will be measured by new metrics. Chapter Eight in *Next Wave* goes into detail on what this might look like. For our purposes in this book, suffice it to say that as long as we continue to use the old metrics (noses and nickels) to define the success of new models, we will find ourselves being pulled right back into practicing the old model. In general, the old model was laser focused on how many people showed up to hear the pastor preach on Sunday. The new emerging models are more concerned with how many disciples are being made. Sitting in a pew on Sunday may be part of the disciple-making process, but many other actions contribute to robust disciple-making. These other actions must be identified, quantified, and celebrated consistently and vigorously.

The point of this chapter can be summed up in the story of Chad and Annette Smith. Before moving to the Platt Park neighborhood of Denver, Chad was a very successful worship and campus pastor at a mega church on the East Coast. Leaving that familiar context behind, they faithfully followed Jesus into the endeavor of starting a new church in the Platt Park neighborhood. Their intention was to allow the local culture to appropriately influence the "shape" of the new church, but their previous experience with conventional approaches kept pulling them toward models they felt at home with—but were not helpful in their immediate cultural context. After several false starts and a detour back onto the staff of a large conventional church, they landed on creating a network of micro churches based on the insight that the catalyst for a micro church is a resident neighborhood missionary.

I asked Chad to share some of the metrics he uses to gauge the progress of the new church. He held up a huge key ring with at least twenty sets of keys on the circle of metal. "One of our favorite metrics is 'How many keys do we have to our neighbor's homes?' When a neighbor trusts us enough to give us the keys to their homes, it is just a matter of time before we will have a significant spiritual conversation. The more spiritual conversations we have, the more likely those conversations will become redemptive and we will have the privilege of helping the person to cross the line of faith."

Perhaps when you have completed the reimagine process with the church you lead, you may find the "How many keys?" question to be one of your favorite metrics as well. I hope you will carefully formulate your own metrics to assist you in measuring missional progress. I hope you will discover what effective disciple-making looks like in your divinely ordained sector of His field of harvest. I hope that you will discover the abundant provision available beyond tithes and offerings alone. And I hope the organizational structure that emerges will be engineered to flex with the continuing twists and turns of the twenty-first century.

At this point in the journey, it is time to decide how you want to proceed. We hope you have recognized that there is more than one right answer to how you respond to the growing desire to reimagine the church you lead. One possible response would be to step into a reimagined process that follows the basic framework outlined in this book. Another possibility is that you recognize you are not personally ready to lead a reimagination process and you choose to raise up another person to lead the charge into the future. Yet another possibility is you see the best path forward is to use a modified reimagine journey to intentionally start a new church.

Larry Grawey added these insights for your consideration:

- "Keep in mind that no matter what path you choose, the journey is likely to take longer than you hope. Your timeline to success will likely take years rather than months.

- As you take the long journey of reimagination, do your best not to go alone! Many pastors are on a similar journey, and they can be a rich source of encouragement and partnership as you go. Seek them out. A great place to start is the "Reimagine Church Group" on Next Wave. The Reimagine Church Group is a real-time peer learning community specifically designed for leaders leading on a reimagination journey."

The great news is that any of the above models (or others that you may invent or find) could be the right response to what you've discovered while reading this book. The only wrong response is to just do nothing at all and maintain the status quo. Trying to stay there will guarantee failure. The other paths may end up looking like failure—but they may also end up enabling you and the church you lead to step into alignment with the Mission of Jesus like never before. Please choose that path.

> *Join the Next Wave Community for practical insights into these existing models and sneak peeks at emerging models.*

GOD IS NOT SURPRISED

I'VE GOT SOME GOOD NEWS and some bad news. Here's the good news. The Church is rapidly expanding across the globe. The bad news is that this is true everywhere but in Europe and North America. In 1900, America had one church for every 370 residents. By 2000, that ratio was one church for every 909 residents. According to Daniel Yang, Executive Director of the Wheaton College-based Church Multiplication Institute, the ratio is now only one church to 1000 residents.[23] This story of the shrinking presence of the church is happening despite the fact that over the last twenty-plus years, the starting of new churches has been an increased priority for almost every denomination and network. Thousands of new churches have been started. Hundreds of millions of dollars have been invested in the starting of those churches—and yet the American Church appears to be losing ground. If the trend continues as is, America will have one church for every 1300 people in 2050.

According to Daniel Yang, in order to stop this unfortunate trend, we need a net gain of 2100 churches per year. (Net gain= the number of existing churches minus closed churches plus newly opened churches).

---

23   From a 2022 presentation by Church Multiplication Institute Executive Director Daniel Yang.

Yang cites recent studies to suggest that, on average, about 3700 churches close each year. So just to stay at our current ratio of churches to people, we need to start 5,800 new churches each year. And that was before COVID-19. Church statisticians are still trying to factor in the impact of COVID-19, but we know the pace of closing churches increased during the pandemic years.

For the sake of the mission of Jesus, we cannot afford to passively watch the church listlessly drift in this dangerous direction. Something has to change.

We're all very familiar with the definition of insanity— "doing the same thing you've always done but expecting different results." Status quo strategies won't get us out of the missional quagmire in which we currently wallow. We've got to do things differently.

God is not surprised by any of this. He's got a plan, and God's plans always include us. We are co-laborers together with Him. We already know how God's big story turns out. He wins! But the story is not finished yet, and God is calling us to join him on His mission to seek and save the lost. He's not willing that any should perish, so let's make it hard for people to "go to hell." But how?

Here are some steps we can take to turn the trend in the right direction.

1.   Start with prayer. If you have been paying attention, prayer has been woven throughout every chapter of this book. We desperately need divine intervention. The challenges we face are impossible to overcome with human wisdom and strategies alone.

2.   Look for ways to co-labor with God. Only God can do what He can do. But He has given us the opportunity to co-create with him. We do need to do what we can do. This book provides

a framework for co-creating with God. He will provide the wisdom to formulate a ministry strategy that complements the miracles that He is working in the world.

3. Let go of habits that are keeping you stuck. Prayer changes things. God changes things. He makes things new. Stop holding on to ways of being the Church that God is calling you to move on from. This is a new wineskins moment. Old wineskins are not bad—they are just incapable of holding the new wine that God is pouring out.

4. Go back to the first chapter of this book and begin walking through the process of reimagining the church.

The practical outcome of the above steps will be fewer churches closed and more new churches opened. But this can only happen if individual leaders choose to step into a process of reimagining the church. The truth is, the only leader whose behavior we have the power to change is us. I am the individual leader who must choose to step into a process of reimagining the church. You are the individual leader who must choose to step into a process of reimagining the church.

Start at the beginning… be the change.

What are you waiting for?

Don't ride the *next wave* of ministry alone.

Reimagine your ministry with Next Wave's real-time learning community for faith leaders like you. See how God uses your tenacious faith to reach new people in new ways. Share your struggles. Celebrate your successes. All inside the Next Wave Community.

SAMPLE MOU
MEMORANDUM OF UNDERSTANDING
BETWEEN
Established Church (Lead Pastor John Doe)
and Reimagined Church
(Jim Johnson)
Anytown, OR

I. PURPOSE

The purpose of this Memorandum of Understanding (MOU) is to provide a frame of reference in which Established Church Lead Pastor John Doe and Jim Johnson, "Reimagined Church Pastor" will outline the details, responsibilities, commitments, timing and requirements in the formation of the "Reimagined Church." With this document, both parties seek to agree to work together in the process of forming, planting, pastoring, and running the subject "Reimagined Church" along with all parties' responsibilities.

II. MISSION

Established Church (EC)

Established Church has been serving the spiritual needs of the Anytown community for over thirty years. Established Church's mission is to make disciples that Love, Make Disciples and Serve.

1. Its vision is to envision Gospel Transformation in individuals, Communities, and the world.

2. Its core values are Biblical, Diversity, Unity, Community, Missional, and Excellence.

The Reimagined Church (RC)

The RC will be a missional community of disciples that will embrace the mission, vision and core values of Established Church. The Reimagined Church will be formed and situated in Anytown. Both Parties will meet together and continue to discuss the best possible location and church property.

III. Description of Partnership

Both EC (Pastor John Doe) and RC (Jim Johnson) have worked together to create this MOU describing the multiple conversations, terms of their mutual collaboration and next steps to begin the Reimagined Church.

Origin of the coordinated effort

1. In the Fall of 2018, Jim Johnson met with a skilled facilitator and Pastor John Doe, Lead Pastor from Established Church. During the meeting, they discussed the next steps to begin drafting an MOU and explore the possibility of launching a New Campus in Anytown. It was agreed that Jim and a skilled facilitator would meet to draft such proposal.

2. In further discussions with a skilled facilitator and Jim Johnson, the original MOU draft was reviewed and a few recommendations were made to address the specific needs and approaches of a Reimagined Church.

3. It was also agreed that both Jim and his wife attend the meeting with Pastor John Doe and a skilled facilitator to review the MOU Agreement.

4. After multiple back and forth conversations, Pastor John Doe offered to Jim Johnson the option to become the Campus Pastors for the Reimagined Church. Established Church (EC) is seeking to target a launch date to be mutually agreed upon.

5. Jim and Sandra Johnson accepted Proposal and decided to move forward with this MOU.

As a result of the offer, EC/Pastor John Doe and Jim Johnson have agreed on the following assumptions and expectations.

A. Assumptions and expectations regarding ministry style and practices.

- EC has specific expectations on the RC regarding worship style and ministry methodology: to be contemporary and relevant to the community it's reaching.
- Campus Pastor will intentionally work with Lead Pastor and Staff to maintain unity and integration with EC Vision, Mission, and Core Values.
- Worship style:
  - Established Church has a creative contemporary worship style with a multi-ethnic expression.

- ○ The Campus will reflect this worship style.
- ○ Services should be well balanced, including time for singing, prayer, altar experience and the preaching/teaching of the word.
- ○ The worship experience will be adjusted to reflect the unique cultural expression of the New community while maintaining a spiritually healthy balance.
- EC Multi-ethnic Ministry
  - ○ Translations on Sundays will continue at 11 E. Fairview Avene for three months and evaluated based on demand and need.
  - ○ New visitors will be provided Reimagined Church details and invited to visit, attend, and participate.
- DISCIPLE-MAKING University and Bible Studies will be offered through New Campus.
- ESL program will continue to be led by EC Director. Reimagined Church Pastor will attend periodically to meet students.
- Ministry methodology
  - ○ The Reimagined Church will begin immediately with the building of a relational network as guided by the principles of Urban Islands Project: Awareness, Connections, Relations, and Discipleship.

B. The Reimagined Church will be formed in three phases:

1. Prelaunch phase (six to nine months):
    - Start Team will be selected and formed by the Campus Pastor. They will be recruited to focus on building the relational network.
    - Ministry Teams will be recruited in cooperation with EC. Ministry team protocol will be in alignment with EC values. Ministry Team leaders will be expected to participate in the outreach start team of the campus. (Examples of teams will be Creative Arts, Children's ministry, Discipleship, Disciple Making University, One Groups, etc.)
    - Ministry Team Leaders organizational structure will be under a Matrix Reporting in which they will be held accountable, lead, and be under the Campus Pastor while working in partnership with BOAG Ministry Staff/Directors.
    - Support Teams will be provided by EC at their discretion. (Example of support teams: administration, child care, security, finance, ushers, etc.)
    - The Campus Pastor will err on the side of over-communicating between leadership and support.
    - RC will have freedom to provide culturally sensitive and informed events to reach community and members (Marriage ministry, Family Camp/Retreat, Women's and Men's Conference, etc.)

2. Launch phase (September/October 2019)
   - Launch will be confirmed once Start Team meets Exposure, Network, and Relationships Goals.
   - PreLaunch Monthly Events will take place three months before official Launch Day.

3. Post-launch phase:

   Reimagined Church will utilize the Established Church discipleship programs and ministry processes. The Campus will reflect the Established Church culture and will be allowed to adjust its approach in order to reflect the unique culture of the New community.

C. Campus Expectations

1. The Campus may not add new ministry programs that are not part of the EC system. But the Campus Pastor may suggest new ministry ideas to be adopted by the EC family of churches.

2. Campus Pastor will teach one of the Disciple Making University classes while developing other teachers.

3. Campus will have DISCIPLE MAKING University and Small Groups patterned after the EC model.

4. These will be under the leadership of the Campus Pastor and in partnership with the EC Ministry Directors through a matrix reporting line.

5. Sunday services:
   - Campus pastor will be responsible for the weekly order of service and serve as the primary weekly communicator from the platform. He will be the face of the campus.

- Campus Pastor will preach at least three times per month with the opportunity to preach more times if applicable. The preaching topic will be determined in consultation with the Lead Pastor.
- Campus Pastor will have the option of preaching series and theme from Lead Pastor and also the flexibility to recommend and preach own series based on needs of Reimagined Church and community.
- Campus Pastor will be allowed to invite guest speakers and music ministers with the consent of Lead Pastor.
- Lead Pastor and Campus Pastor will agree on Service times.
- Services at Reimagined Church will not be canceled or changed without consent from Campus Pastor.

D. Assumptions and expectations regarding finances and financial management.

1. Transition process, timeline, and income expectations:

   a. Phase I: PreLaunch and Launch (0–12 months): Bi-vocational, attend Staff Meetings once a month remotely via Zoom, determine minimum hours and potential income.

   b. Phase II: Launch and Post-Launch (12-18 months): Review and Evaluate Campus. Bi-vocational.

   c. Phase III (18-24 months): Review and Evaluate Campus and MOU Agreement.

2. Financial management details
    - A job description will be created, and minimum hours of focus will be determined.
    - During bi-vocational status, Campus Pastor will reserve the right to vacations and holidays in accordance with his profession and career. To be revisited at time of full-time staff discussions.
    - Initially, EC will assume all Operating Expenses, including all equipment expenses, marketing, and any rental or property management expenses related to the subject campus.
    - EC will handle all personnel expenses. Any current or future Salary discussions will be updated upon further discussions with Lead Pastor John Doe and Jim Johnson.
    - As RC grows, staff should be hired to support the Campus. Hiring decisions and approval process will be agreed with Pastor John, Campus Pastor, and EC Board.
    - Reimagined Church Pastor's Wife, Sandra Johnson, can be considered for part-time staff role as campus grows and develops.
    - EC will cover all administrative expenses.
    - All income received (donations, tithes, and offerings) by RC will flow and be deposited into EC Ledger Account. EC will provide all accounting services, reporting, and details for RC and tracked as Campus financial entry.
    - RC may be offered opportunities for investment, such as purchasing a property, etc. EC Lead Pastor John Doe, the church's board, and Campus Pastor Jim Johnson will handle all acquisitions.

- EC will provide Campus Pastor with a corporate credit card that will allow the Campus Pastor to make purchases on behalf of the campus. Budget and guidelines for such purchases will be determined by EC.
- Campus Pastor will create a proposed budget for the start-up and operation of the campus by an agreed-upon date yet to be determined.
- A subsequent conversation will occur regarding how the new startup will continue to be funded.

E. Assumptions and expectations regarding governance.

1. Campus Pastor will be considered equal to the other Staff Pastors concerning role and authority. His goal is to oversee the campus and its operation. The whole campus team will report to the campus pastor, and campus Pastor will report directly to the Lead Pastor but will work with the other ministry/staff pastors to seek support, assistance, and resources.

2. Campus Pastor and Lead Pastor will meet at least once per month to relationally connect. Campus Pastor is responsible for scheduling that meeting. Additionally, either Lead Pastor or Campus Pastor may agree to invite a skilled facilitator or outside assistance to assist them in maintaining agreement and clarity.

3. Campus Pastor will participate in all EC regular weekly staff meetings as permitted by his current profession. Initially, the Campus Pastor will be bi-vocational, and EC understands that the Campus Pastor might not be able to attend some events or meetings.

4. EC staff will be oriented to the principles of Urban Islands Project to help them be in alignment with the start-up processes of the Reimagined Church.

5. Campus Pastor to attend Board Meeting twice a year to provide update, review Results, and make budget recommendations.

6. Campus Pastor will preach at least three times per month with the opportunity to preach more times if applicable. The preaching topic will be determined in consultation with the Lead Pastor.

7. If Campus Pastor receives invitations to preach in other churches, retreats, and conferences, he may do so with consent from Lead Pastor and Campus Service is organized. Lead Pastor should be informed in advance of these opportunities. Campus Pastor may retain any honorariums as personal income received.

8. EC intends to have the following categories of affiliated churches.
   - EC Campuses: never intend to go sovereign (but may)
   - EC Satellite Churches: might go sovereign
   - EC Network Churches: already established churches that come under the wing of EC.
   - EC Church Plant: Sovereign in governance and finances from day one.

9. RC will be considered an EC Campus for governance purposes, and it will be known publicly as one of the EC locations.

10. In case Lead Pastor John Doe is no longer in this same position, Campus Pastor and Reimagined Church has option of becoming a Sovereign Church.

11. RC staff and family members may join the EC health insurance plan if it is advantageous for them. EC will be responsible for the payment of insurance premiums.

12. General liability insurance will be covered under the insurance umbrella of EC

13. EC will determine all salaries and all staffing decisions in conjunction with Campus Pastor.

14. RC will not need a constitution and bylaws, and it will be under the constitution and bylaws of EC. The need for a separate constitution and bylaws will be considered only if the RC becomes sovereign at some point in the future.

15. The Campus Pastor will be committing to the RC for at least three years, and the commitment will be reviewed once every year.

F. Assumptions and expectations regarding ethics.

1. Campus Pastor has complete freedom to invite other members/leaders from EC to serve on the RC team.

2. RC will be known to the EC community as a campus of EC.

3. Protocol for recruiting team members
   - Campus Pastor is empowered to recruit anyone to serve on the campus outreach, ministry, and support teams.
   - Campus Pastor will review names with Lead Pastor.
   - The Campus team will report to the Campus Pastor under the authority of the Lead Pastor. Campus Pastor will recruit and form a new team dedicated to the RC to come alongside and guided by the Urban Islands Cohort church planting principles. This will allow the team to be missional and assist the Campus pastor in the outreach and church planting activities that will be put in place for the first 12 to

24 months of the satellite development. This will allow the Campus Pastor to recruit current members of EC from the different ministries of the church.

G. Assumptions and expectations regarding metrics and timeline

1. Metrics will be developed in consultation with Urban Islands Project.

2. In this timeline, our monthly metrics will be reviewed and updated based on progress and work done by the Start Team.

3. The Urban Islands Project Missional Metrics will be used as a baseline. The launch day target number will be 120. The aspirational launch date is to be determined. Both the start target number and start date may be amended through agreement of Campus Pastor and Lead Pastor.

4. Potential Timeline:
    *   Present and Announce to Church: 6 months from now
    *   Start Team 10 members: 8 months from now
    *   Start Team 20 members: 12 months from now
    *   200 Relationships: 15 months from now

IV. SUMMARY

RC will be a satellite campus under the legal and organizational umbrella of EC. The relationship between EC and RC will be reviewed annually based on the assumptions and expectations described in this memorandum.

V. EFFECTIVE DATE

This memorandum becomes effective on the date it is signed by Pastor John Doe and Pastor Jim Johnson.

_____   _____

Pastor Jim Johnson   Pastor John Doe
Campus Pastor   Lead Pastor
Reimagined Church   Established Church
Date _____   Date _____
Jjohson456@gmail.com   jdoe@EstablishedChurch.org

www.ingramcontent.com/pod-product-compliance
Lightning Source LLC
Chambersburg PA
CBHW031504120626
46545CB00005B/1743